Charles Edward Smith

The World Lighted

A study of the Apocalypse

Charles Edward Smith

The World Lighted
A study of the Apocalypse

ISBN/EAN: 9783744719247

Printed in Europe, USA, Canada, Australia, Japan

Cover: Foto ©Lupo / pixelio.de

More available books at **www.hansebooks.com**

THE WORLD LIGHTED,

A STUDY OF THE APOCALYPSE.

BY

CHARLES EDWARD SMITH,
AUTHOR OF
"THE BAPTISM IN FIRE."

FUNK & WAGNALLS.

NEW YORK:
18 & 20 ASTOR PLACE.

1890

LONDON:
44 FLEET STREET.

All Rights Reserved.
PRINTED IN THE UNITED STATES.

PREFACE.

It is surely not a situation to be regarded with complacency by the Christian world that one of the principal books of the Bible yet remains for the most part uncomprehended and practically useless. It ought to be a matter of additional grief that a conviction of the impossibility of understanding the book has come to exist, like that which we feel about reaching the North Pole. The consequence is that any hardy explorer who ventures to attempt the opening up of its mysteries is likely to encounter such a condemnatory and disparaging prejudgment of his undertaking as any one would now meet with who should propose to follow in the footsteps of Franklin, Kane, and De Long.

The cause of this state of things is obviously very similar to that which has made further Arctic exploration so unpopular. The world is tired of reading the painful story of the baffled navigator, who pays with his life for his temerity in endeavoring to penetrate the secrets of the North. And the Church is tired of reading the guesses of expounders who have essayed to grapple with the perplexities of the Apocalypse, only to show how profoundly difficult the undertaking is, and how unequal to it are those who have attempted it. For a new venture to be made into this *terra in-*

cognita of Scripture seems, as a matter of course, only another display of foolhardiness.

We ought, however, not to permit ourselves to feel thus, or to treat with cold distrust any honest endeavor to find out what the Revelation means. It is not necessary to find the North Pole, but it is necessary for the Church to understand the Apocalypse. It was given that it might be understood—understood sufficiently to bring it within the description of "all Scripture" which "is given by inspiration of God, and is *profitable* for doctrine, for reproof, for correction, for instruction in righteousness, that the man of God may be perfect, thoroughly furnished unto all good works." The man of God is not furnished as he ought to be until he knows more about the Apocalypse. No matter how many investigators have prophecy may be ended, and that the wonderful knowledge and help which it undoubtedly contains may become the available possession of the Church, are certainly sufficient motives to attempt again the explanation of the prophecy, and yet again, until that explanation is found conclusively.

The present writer, then, begs that the contribution which he seeks to make to this great enterprise be received not only with civility, but with sympathy and good-will. He hopes that he is not one of those singular spirits to whom the very impossibility of an undertaking constitutes its irresistible charm. He is

CONTENTS.

	PAGE
PREFACE	iii
I. FINDING THE KEY	9
II. THE KEY	15
III. IS THIS WORLD TO BE LIGHTED UP?	28
IV. THE EPISTLES TO THE SEVEN CHURCHES	41
V. HEAVEN THE SOURCE OF LIGHT	51
VI. THE OPENING OF THE SEVEN SEALS	62
VII. THE FOUR TRUMPETS	75
VIII. THE FIFTH AND SIXTH TRUMPETS	90
IX. THE VISION OF THE TRUTH	99
X. THE CHURCH AND THE WORLD	105
XI. THE CHURCH AND THE DRAGON	118
XII. THE WILD BEASTS	133
XIII. THE FORCES OF ILLUMINATION	141
XIV. THE ERA OF JUDGMENTS	152
XV. THE SEVEN VIALS	160
XVI. THE SCARLET WOMAN	172
XVII. THE FALL OF BABYLON	180
XVIII. THE PREMILLENNIAL AGE	188
XIX. THE MILLENNIUM	199
XX. THE NEW JERUSALEM	209

THE WORLD LIGHTED.

I.

FINDING THE KEY.

It is a surprising fact that, although almost two thousand years of the Christian era have gone, no one has yet discovered the key to the Apocalypse—that is to say, no one has succeeded in getting such a general conception of the purpose of the book as would make it generally intelligible. It cannot truthfully be said that this has yet been done. The utmost that any commentator has accomplished, so far, is to elucidate passages of the book by what seem more like happy guesses at its meaning, than interpretations founded upon the sure basis of a clear perception of the leading purpose of the Apocalypse.

Perhaps some modification of the apparently sweeping character of this denial ought to be made. It ought to be admitted that even the unlearned reader, if he be a sincere Christian, can find, and does find, occasional passages in it of which he has some not doubtful idea of the meaning. The Revelation of John is the Rocky Mountain region of the Scriptures, in which even the most untutored wanderer comes to the loveliest valleys nestling here and there, and stands now and then upon a peak of vision which gives him a broad and inspiring view. At the same time, such wanderers have to confess that they are wanderers; that of the general topography of this strange country they know nothing whatever; and that, to their minds, it yet lies in the utter confusion of a primeval wilderness that has never been explored, surveyed, or mapped. There is probably no book of the Bible regarding which the ordinary reader feels so hopeless of ever having any lucid idea. It is not so very different with the extraordinary readers. Even to these the Apocalypse yet remains an Africa, a comparatively unknown continent. Like Africa, it is true, this book is being opened up by exploration; the sources of the Nile, the Congo region, large sections here and there must now be admitted to be understood, and yet, in the absence of any comprehensive notion of the general purport of the Apocalypse, it must be confessed yet to await the discoverer who shall throw light upon its principal obscurities.

Is there, then, no key, or has it been lost beyond recovery? Did the Author of the Bible intend to make this last book so dark that its purport should remain perpetually an enigma? Has He hidden the key so that it cannot be found? Ought the failure of so many great and good men to find it to make us all feel that it would be presumption to look further? Or may we say, the key can be found; it was intended by God that it should be found. The audacity of one who looks for it, and who thinks that he has found it, may be only the "eureka" of every discoverer who finds that regarding which everybody wonders, when it is brought to light, that he did not see it himself?

Supposing now that we have courage enough to look for this key, let us consider (as we should) where it may probably be. Are any considerations likely to be derived from other books of the Bible which would aid us in forming an opinion as to the probable character of the last book? Would the book itself be likely to contain a clew to its own meaning? If so, what part of the book? Would the door of a house be a proper place in which to expect to find the key? Would the beginning and introduction of the Apocalypse be likely to contain some sufficient hints as to the nature of what follows? Asking ourselves such questions as these, we shall, I think, be able to answer them unhesitatingly. Notwithstanding the fact that so much previous study has yielded so little profit; notwithstanding the fact that better men than ourselves have been baffled; nevertheless we cannot help thinking that there is a key, that somebody is going to find it, that that somebody may be one as well as another—anybody who is willing to look—and that he will find it partly by general considerations drawn from other Scriptures, but chiefly by carefully examining the *door* of the Apocalypse—that is, its introduction in the first chapter.

To know where to look is, of course, the greatest possible encouragement that one is going to be able to find anything that has been lost. If we can get any glimmer of probability regarding this matter, we can fall to looking again with a good heart, even after any number of previous failures. It may be well to point out here the fact that there has been, in the minds of previous investigators, little idea that the clew to Revelation was any more likely to be found in one place than in any other.

It is only one of the many signs of the general bewilderment regarding this book that students of it should be so uncertain where to look for its key, and equally ready to expect to find it anywhere. As a general thing they get far on in the study of it before they discover anything that looks to them like a clew. Alford does, indeed, find his supposed clew in the first chapter. But it is not so with most. Dr. Brunson's "Key to the Apocalypse" he discovers in the latter part of the book, in the chapters which relate to the fall of the papacy. Some find the leading conception of the prophecy in that cry for vengeance which is uttered by the souls seen under the altar in the sixth chapter. Renan was so absurd as to claim that his explanation of a passage in the seventeenth chapter, concerning "the beast that was, and is not, and yet is," which he thought had been suggested by what is called the "Nero-fable" of history, is the originating principle of the whole book, the *mere de l'Apocalypse*. I mention but one more, and that the one which I should regard as entitled to the most respect, on account of the general excellence of the work in which it is found. Dr. Justin A. Smith's "Commentary on the Revelation," in the preparation of which he had the scholarly assistance of Dr. Boise, and which had the further advantage of being edited by

Dr. Alvah Hovey, one of the most accomplished of modern biblical investigators, is by far the best commentary on this book with which I am acquainted. I cannot too strongly express my admiration for the great learning, the carefulness and candor, and the extraordinary good sense and sound judgment of the authors of this work. Not having examined it until I had about half completed these studies of my own, I almost thought that my own conclusions had been anticipated, so largely did its interpretations run parallel with mine. I am glad to be able to appeal to such a valuable authority for the corroboration of many of my own views. It seems as if they would all have been anticipated if Dr. Smith and his co-adjutors had had the good fortune to lay hold, at the outset, of the same general conception of the intention of the Apocalypse. The great merits of this work, however, serve to make all the more obvious the common bewilderment as to where the key is likely to be found. For Dr. Smith finds what he calls the "adjusting principle" of the Revelation in an obscure expression of the tenth chapter—viz., "the mystery of God."

Is it likely, I ask, that the Inspirer of the prophecy would have left its readers to stumble on so far through this most labyrinthine of all the Scriptures before the clew to its windings was furnished? Or does it seem more probable that, as Ariadne supplied Theseus with a thread at the very entrance of the cavern which he had to penetrate, so God would put a torch into the hands of His children at the very beginning of their task? There is certainly a very strong probability in favor of a clew thus obtained at the start over one which has to be picked up in some unexpected place far on in the prophecy. Let us look for the key, then, somewhere in the first chapter!

II.

THE KEY.

He would be a bold man who should say, I am *sure* that I have found the key to the meaning of the Apocalypse. Where so many have tried and failed, where the wisest and most trusted venture only with hesitation, it would be presumptuous to tread except with utmost modesty and entire freedom from a dogmatic spirit. But since no view of this remarkable book yet commands general acceptance, it is still open to any investigator to find a better one. Over the portals of the prophecy is inscribed a blessing upon him " that readeth" and them " that hear" its words. That is a divine invitation to try to find the lost key. The motive is a great one. He who succeeds in this search will be so happy as to open the meaning of this book as it was never opened before. Even though one should fail, he may at least hope to belong to a not ignoble company of reverent scholars, each of whom has flashed the light of his torch upon some of the dark places in this most difficult book of the Bible.

The key to the Apocalypse is such a general conception of its purpose as will enable us to see the harmony of its various parts with that conception. No such " adjusting principle" has ever yet been demonstrated, and hence we have no such key. I have mentioned several ideas which have been suggested as having been formative in the production of the book, but it remains to be shown that any one of them deserves this high credit. I do not think that it can be shown. For that purpose it would be necessary to go through the Apocalypse, and find its parts all springing from such a germinal idea. I do not know that the sponsors for these various conceptions have even attempted such a task. But they cannot know that they are correct without attempting it.

When Newton hit upon the idea of gravitation, it was found to agree with all the facts of astronomy so universally and so minutely that nobody could doubt its truth. The key fitted all the wards in the lock, and was demonstrated to belong to it beyond question. Is there such a general conception of the intention and plan of this book as will fit its various parts and representations, and thus prove itself to be the divine idea according to which this most ingenious and intricate literary production is constructed? This, and nothing less than this, must be our task: first to find that which looks like a key in the very place where a key ought to be, and then to prove our finding by going through the whole structure and unlocking every door. When we have done that we shall be quite sure that we have the key.

Our first inquiry must be, What is there in the introductory chapter of Revelation which may probably be the clew to the plan of the entire book?

To settle this question, let the reader go over and over the chapter until all its prominent thoughts have been grasped. As I have done this there has gradually been made to stand out before my mind, against the background of the remainder of the chapter, that remarkable vision described in the last seven verses. All that goes before leads up to this. Dwelling long enough upon its details for the imagination to place them before the mind's eye, one at length beholds, as John did, a magnificent array of *light-bearers.* "*Seven golden candlesticks.*" "Seven stars." "THE SUN!"

I acknowledge that I have separated these expressions from their connections, but I have done so because it seems to me that in looking at the connections we lose sight of the more important things connected. Having once seen that these luminaries are all there, there is no objection to restoring the connecting words. None of those words in the least impair the effect of the impression which has been gained by first looking at the luminaries alone. The seven candlesticks are none the less candlesticks that "one like unto the Son of man" is in the midst of them. The seven stars are none the less stars that they are in the right hand of the Son of man. The sun is none the less a sun that it is the countenance of the same majestic figure of which it is said that "His countenance was as the sun shineth in his strength." * The more one reflects upon this chapter, the more he will feel that its most salient feature is this vision of light-bearers, and that this vision must have a natural and easily understood significance, which is intended to suggest the purport of the entire book.

---

* "Not the countenance, but the appearance in general ;" "The entire form appears as surrounded with the brilliancy of the sun" (Düsterdieck *in loco,* with whom best commentators agree).

Regarding this sublime vision Dr. Justin A. Smith remarks profoundly : " Rich as the Bible is in vision, symbol, and allegory, it is perhaps impossible to name any passage which in suggestiveness, alike sublime and tender, surpasses or even equals this, in which Jesus in glory appears to John in the desolation of his exile." If that be a just estimate, and it undoubtedly is, why is not this passage worthy to furnish the key to the Apocalypse ? And yet nobody seems to have thought of it as such. It has been passed over as having no special significance growing out of its prominence as the first vision in a book of visions, and students have looked anywhere and everywhere else to find the germinal idea of the book.

It cannot be an accident that the Apocalypse is placed last of all the books of the Bible. It is last because it has a fitness to be last ; it was divinely intended to end the sacred volume. Many have noticed that the Paradise which was lost in Genesis is regained in Revelation, and that other types found in the first book of the Scriptures reappear in the last book. Fewer have observed the completeness of this circle of divine thought. What is the first type of all ? Is it not *light*, coming to displace the darkness which was upon the face of the deep ? Does not the sublime fiat, " Let there be light !" stand at the very threshold of inspiration, as if to announce the dawn not only of light physical, but also of light spiritual ? What is inspiration, what is any truth, but light* for

---

* That light symbolizes truth in the Scriptures may almost be taken for granted. It is, at any rate, the predominant idea : Psalm 43 : 3, " O send out Thy light and Thy truth !" Psalm 119 :

man's mental darkness? If now Holy Writ complete the cycle of revelation, it will end, as it begins, with *light;* with the completion of the purpose of God announced at the outset to give spiritual light to the world. The Apocalypse probably belongs at the end of the canon because, and only because, it tells how God will carry out to the full His great intention to shed truth upon mankind.

Having thus indicated to the reader what I regard as the seminal principle of the book, I wish to consider another and rival claim. I refer to that of Dean Alford. No other which I have seen demands consideration here, because no other has been found in the place where I have contended that the key ought to be found. But Alford also finds his clew in the first chapter, in one of the opening verses of the chapter—" Behold, *He cometh with clouds;* and every eye shall see Him, and they also which pierced Him: and all kindreds of the earth shall wail because of Him. Even so, Amen." Taking this passage with other similar passages of the book, especially some of its closing words, Dean Alford decides that the subject of the book must be the second, and personal, and glorious coming of our Lord.

105, " Thy word is a light unto my path ;" Proverbs 6 : 23, " The law is light ;" 1 John 1 : 5, " God is light, and in Him is no darkness at all." Alford comments, "He is the Fountain of light material and light ethical. In the one world darkness is the absence of light ; in the other, darkness, *untruthfulness, deceit, falsehood,* is the absence of God." " Of the ethical darkness here denied, the Schol. says, ' Neither ignorance, nor deceit, nor sin, nor death.' " See also Bernard's definition of light in his " Progress of Doctrine in the New Testament," pp. 116, 117.

Positive as he feels, however, about this conclusion, it does not appear to have served him very much as a key to the contents of the prophecy. He confesses upon many a page of his exposition that he is wholly at a loss in seeking for an intelligible meaning. If he is to be believed, all interpreters before himself have been betrayed into many blunders, and have only here and there got a momentary glimpse of the intent of the book. His own chief claim is that he has laid hold of certain fundamental facts which must be used in threading the labyrinth of the prophecy. The principal of these facts is that the book treats of the second and personal coming of the Lord Jesus Christ. But it must be confessed that this guiding principle did not serve Alford very well; we know that from his own frequent acknowledgment. He seems to think that he has a key, and yet is unable to open many of the doors. He might almost as well have no key at all.

It must be admitted, nevertheless, that the prominence of the passage and the impressiveness of the words from which Alford derives his idea seem to demand for them some considerable part in determining the subject-matter of the book. The question is not whether the passage is important, but whether Alford has correctly defined its importance. Is he justified in at once taking it for granted that the passage relates, and relates solely, to the coming of our Lord in glory? Admit that the words contain a sweep of prophetic vision which extends on to the final conclusion of all things. But may they not also include a suggestion of some other and intermediate "coming," which is rather to be considered the main subject of the book? The question is how we are to interpret the language, and whether the vision which follows it is not to be regarded as a more explicit indication of the kind of coming intended. In a word, does not the vision compel us to decide that it is Christ's coming *in His truth*, and as *the Truth*, which is meant rather than, or, perhaps, as the grand preparation required for, His coming in His glory?

To settle this question it is not enough to appeal to the numerous instances in which a coming of Christ of *some sort* is referred to. The New Testament speaks of many comings of many kinds. Great confusion of thought arises from a failure to discriminate these various kinds of comings from one another. Bishop Merrill, in his work on the "Second Coming of Christ," points out a distinction which ought to be made in the gospels between Christ's coming *in His kingdom* and His coming *in His glory*. If this be a legitimate distinction it clears up a good deal of apparent conflict between passages which treat of the second coming; but Alford has quite failed to grasp any such distinction. References to Christ's coming in His kingdom he applies to His personal coming. But in so doing he makes a mistake which is fatal, in my judgment, to a correct interpretation of the Apocalypse.

The coming of Christ in this book was to be a *speedy* coming. "Behold, I come quickly!" To assert this to be true of Christ's coming in His glory, and to say that any coming, at however remote a date, is to be regarded as speedy, is to say that words have been used out of their meaning. The prophecy was of things that were *shortly* to come to pass, and Christ's personal coming is yet, for aught that we know, far in the distance. "They also which pierced Him" were to see this coming, reminding us of our Lord's own prediction that He was to come before some who heard Him speak should "taste of death." To the high-priest He said, "Hereafter ye shall see the Son of man sitting on the right hand of power, and coming in the clouds of heaven." This language admits of a double explanation, the coming of Christ at the Judgment and His coming in the progress of His religion, and in the overthrow of Judaism, even in the high-priest's lifetime. The difficulty which we feel in applying terms of haste to the personal coming of our Lord disappears when we think of His coming in the truth, which, if we consider the difficulties in its way, has made rapid progress.

"Behold, He cometh with clouds!" Is not this the description of Christ's personal coming? Not necessarily. The expression is the connecting link between the Apocalypse and Daniel's vision of the coming kingdom of heaven, in his seventh chapter. In that vision, while the earthly kingdoms were represented by wild beasts coming up from below, the kingdom of heaven was represented by "one like unto the Son of man, coming in the clouds of heaven." The clouds above are the opposite of the sea below. They denote the heavenly and divine origin of this kingdom in contrast with the earthly and diabolic sources of the kingdoms which it is to conquer. The Son of man is the opposite of the beasts, indicating that the kingdom of heaven is to be human, and rational, and godlike rather than beastly, and irrational, and devilish. That the reign portrayed is not Christ's personal reign, at least upon earth, is distinctly affirmed. Again and again we are assured that "the kingdom is to be given to the saints of the Most High." What Daniel taught by the vision of the Son of man coming in the clouds of heaven is the progress of the Church in subduing and ruling over the world.

Now what this expression meant in Daniel it may mean in Revelation. May we not speak more strongly, and say that it does probably mean the same thing in one book that it does in the other? The two books are essentially of the same kind; not only here, but elsewhere, the Apocalypse takes up the symbolism of Daniel and uses it and extends it. The two books might almost be considered two volumes of the same book. If now the symbolism of the Son of man coming in the clouds of heaven is not to be taken so much as a definite portrait of Christ and a picture of a single event in His history as a figurative representation of His Church and its fortunes; if, I say, this be its meaning in Daniel, why should it not be its meaning in Revelation? Certainly this is the most reasonable interpretation. Beginning to interpret in this way at the outset of the book, we shall avoid making caricatures of our Lord and of His history farther on, into which the literal method of interpretation would lead us. We get our first all-important hint as to the nature of the book which we are studying, that everywhere it is symbolism that we must expect, and not realistic portraits and definite statements.

The Apocalypse, then, takes up Daniel's revelation concerning the kingdom of heaven upon earth, and carries it further. What does it add, here in this first chapter, foreshadowing what is to come through the whole book? It adds many things, but the chief of them is that the kingdom of heaven is a *kingdom of light*. Daniel did not tell how the saints of the Most High were to come into the possession of their kingdom. But the Apocalypse tells here upon its first page. It says that they are to get their kingdom *by shining*. For how does the vision of the Son of man, beheld by John, differ from that seen by Daniel? The answer is the key to the meaning of the Apocalypse. Strange that so little heed should have been taken of this difference, and of its bearing upon the interpretation of the entire book. The Son of man now has an appearance like *the sun*, holds in His right hand *seven stars*, and stands in the midst of *seven golden candlesticks*. The sun, the stars, the candlesticks—all are light-bearers. Is it possible to escape the significance of these symbols? What do they mean, what else can they mean, but that the chief characteristic of the kingdom of heaven upon earth is that it is a kingdom of light, and that the chief means by which this kingdom is to extend itself is the impartation of truth, until all error is destroyed and knowledge everywhere prevails? Is not this grand illumination, with which the book opens, a prophecy and a promise that the whole of this dark world is to be lighted up with "the knowledge of the glory of God in the face of Jesus Christ"?

There is another most significant item in the description of the Son of man. Out of His proceeds a sharp sword. As a portrait this is grotesque, but as symbolism it is noble and intelligible. For we know what this sword is; it is the "Word of God," which is "sharper than a two-edged sword, piercing even to the dividing asunder of soul and spirit, and of the joints and marrow, and is a discerner of the thoughts and intents of the heart." We are reminded also of that sublime apostrophe in one of the Messianic psalms (the 45th), "Gird Thy sword upon thy thigh, O most mighty, with Thy glory and Thy majesty. And in Thy majesty ride prosperously *because of truth* and meekness and righteousness." Consider now the force of these combined symbols, found upon what may be called the title-page of the Apocalypse, or in the prologue of the dramatic action afterward to be described. Do they not beyond question inform us that the whole book relates to the progress of *truth* in enlightening the moral darkness of the world, and that the wars therein described are the wars between truth and error, and the victory the victory of complete and universal knowledge over all ignorance and so over all sin?

I propose, then, this conception—*The Progress of Truth in Enlightening and Saving Mankind*—as the fundamental idea of the Apocalypse, and the key to the meaning of its symbols. I believe that this idea applied to the various parts of the book introduces an order and makes possible a harmony never before found by any system of interpretation. With this clew I do not despair of being able to make even him who sits in the room of the unlearned feel that he has a pretty clear and decidedly delightful conception of what the Apocalypse means.

There is still another direction in which confirmation may be obtained before we proceed further. There are other facts which create expectation that a *denouement* of this kind would be the conclusion of the inspired volume. If the victory of truth be the last word of revelation, we might expect to find waymarks leading up to this close. So we do. The careful reader of John's epistles will find much in them about truth, *the* truth. There is not much else in the short second and third epistles. The first one opens with the message that "God is light, and in Him is no darkness at all," and closes with the emphasis to be placed upon the facts of Christian knowledge. Jude's message is the necessity of contending earnestly for the faith once delivered unto the saints. It is as if those who were appointed to utter the closing words of the Bible realized especially the immense importance of right doctrine in the great struggle before the Church. These apostles laid increased emphasis upon correct Christian ideas, and called the children of God to be clear and positive and scriptural in all their teachings. One who notes these signs will not be surprised when he finds that the very last book of the Bible is devoted to a description, by means of symbols, of the great war between God's truth and the devil's lies, and the picturing of the glorious results when truth shall have done its perfect work.

If this idea of the book be the correct one, it must have a radical effect upon our method of interpretation. We are relieved from the necessity of identifying the conflicts described with any of the material conflicts of history. Under the cover of such warring, and of other material phenomena, the Holy Spirit has really described the long war between truth and error. It is, perhaps, the only method that could have been taken. The actual war of ideas, of right doctrine with false doctrine, of sound knowledge with human fancies and prejudices and perversions, could hardly have been literally set forth. It was set forth under the symbolism of battle, and blood, and fire, and earthquakes, and portents and prodigies in heaven and earth far beyond what any human imagination could have invented. As we read the descriptions we are to be thinking of the great spiritual conflict, which is the real one. Not that this does not involve and imply the other, or that sometimes the literal shock of arms may not be discovered and, perhaps, identified. But this identification is not essential to our having a fairly clear idea of the purport of what we are reading. It is not necessary to be so thoroughly versed in European history as to be able to select among its numberless details that one which was of sufficient importance to be predicted by inspiration. The general truth conveyed concerning the great struggle of light with darkness, and its successive stages, reverses, and victories, may be distinctly seen, and assurance grow as the prophecy proceeds that while smoke covers the conflict and hides its exact details, the right is winning the day and may count upon complete triumph.

III.

IS THIS WORLD TO BE LIGHTED UP?

BEFORE I proceed further to trace and test the idea which has been presented as the formative principle of the Apocalypse, it seems to me proper and, indeed, necessary, to stop and consider what kind of an idea it is. We should not be warranted in spending our time in pursuit of this conception unless it is a conception worthy of the high place which is claimed for it. Is it worthy of that place, worthy to be the subject of the last book of the Bible? Can it be possible that it is the divine intention to light up this cavern of a world until it is as bright spiritually as noonday radiance makes it physically? Is it desirable to do that? Is it necessary? Is it feasible? What kind of an idea is this which the glorious vision of "one like unto the Son of man," as the centre of a spiritual solar system, has suggested to my mind as the subject of this wonderful book?

No one can deny the grandeur of the conception. If any fault can be found with it, it is that it seems too grand ever to be realized. In some other world, perhaps; in the world of the angels; but in this world? It seems far too much to believe. One thinks of the Egyptian darkness which has rested upon the human mind from the beginning; of the Stygian ignorances which yet exist in wide territories of every continent, and asks himself, Will all this be cleared away and displaced by a world-wide intelligence and a world-wide information? Will every man on the globe at length know enough to have his chance of securing his highest interests for time and for eternity? Will the time ever come when some Captain Cook will sail round the globe and touch at no far-off coast or remote island, where correct ideas of the relations between God and man and between man and man are not entertained? Would that it might be! What well-wisher of his race, what lover of this fair planet,

"Where every prospect pleases,
And only man is vile,"

but would be delighted to have it so? What a triumph of Christianity and of civilization that would be! What an honor to Christ it would be! How the bells of eternity would ring at such a consummation! How heaven would rejoice! If we reject the idea it is not because it is not unspeakably glorious, but because we think so much glory cannot possibly be.

But what is the genesis of this idea? Where did it come from? Is it a phantasy of my brain, or of some other brain as disordered as my own? Is it a meteoric intruder into our realm of rational and orderly thought from some region of intellectual vagaries? Or is it a common and familiar idea of the Word of God, and do we think it because God has thought it before us? What did Daniel say? "Many shall run to and fro, and knowledge shall be increased." What did Habakkuk say? "For the earth shall be filled with the knowledge of the glory of the Lord, as the waters cover the sea." It is not, then, my idea, or anybody's, but God's. It is His idea of what it would be well to do, of what He would like to do; yes, and of what He means to do. If He said it in Habakkuk, it is not unlikely that He has said it in Revelation.

There may be those who have thought that Christianity is yet to be universal, who have not quite realized that for this purpose the general enlightenment of mankind is indispensable. The empire of Satan is fortified by ignorance, and to pull down his empire you must first pull down his fortifications. The blank ignorances, the stolid thoughtlessness, the stupid superstitions, the foolish prejudices, the silly trusts, the groundless fears, the misunderstandings, misconceptions, misrepresentations, falsehoods, deceits, impositions—how large a part these have in holding the human race in slavery to the great despot! Sin skulks always behind a lie; evil lives in the shadow of a falsehood; make the lie impossible of credence and the evil would disappear. If the world is ever to be Christianized it must be enlightened. Ignorance, instead of being the "mother of devotion," is the mother of superstition. There is absolutely no way to give the uttermost parts of the earth to the Son for his possession except by the method of Habakkuk. The knowledge of the Lord must fill the earth, as the waters cover the sea. Everywhere men must know too much to trust in fetish, or idol, or priest, or good works, or anything but their Saviour. Perceiving this necessity, and knowing how dark the world was in the first century—nay, how dark it is even now, we shall not think it strange that the last word of Inspiration is a majestic prophecy, showing how God will light up the globe.

But is it feasible? Can it be done? It is a question of light and light-bearers. We cannot tell by looking at the darkness. Darkness looks more invincible than it really is. Bring in the lights, and darkness flees discomfited before them. To think only of the persistence of error, of the obstinacy of prejudice, of the many lives of which a lie seems possessed, so that to kill it once and again is only to see it start up in a new place or a new form; to think how many people the wide world through count it their interest to keep the falsehoods alive and the truths out of sight; to think how long the present degree of enlightenment has been in coming, is to be discouraged and hopeless. But still if we could but have light enough we should be able to light up the whole dark world. Have we light enough? Has God Himself light enough to banish the spiritual darkness of our planet? The answer is upon the very title-page of the Apocalypse. That is what its first vision seems to mean. Seven candlesticks; seven stars; the sun—is it not enough? We have only to consider the light-bearers at our disposal to be assured that the task can be accomplished.

First, let us consider the ultimate significance of the fact that there are in the world institutions which Inspiration has thought worthy to symbolize by the term "candlesticks," or, as it might better be translated, lamp-stands. The original of the figure is, of course, the seven-branched candlestick, or light-holder, of the tabernacle. This was a type of the light-giving quality of the modern Church—that is, its teaching power, its ability to instruct and educate mankind. The seven golden candlesticks represent the Church as God sees it, in its knowledge of the truth as it is in Jesus, and its adaptation to the task of communicating that knowledge to others. The symbol ought to raise our idea of the prophetic capacity of the Church, as well as instruct us as to what is to be considered the *true* Church of God in the world. It is the Church which knows the most about true religion, and can shine the most brightly on the religious darkness of men, rather than the Church which is most punctilious about ceremonials, and arrogates to itself the most authority. Of this Church, in its adaptation to illuminate the moral darkness of earth, the divine estimate is very high. God feels the same confidence in His ability to light up the world by its means that a man feels who "lights a candle" and setteth it "on a candlestick," that it will give "light unto all that are in the house." In this confidence Jesus said, even to the little company of disciples which stood about Him, "Ye are the light *of the world.*" With a like confidence Paul said to the Philippian Christians, "Ye shine as lights in the world." The vision of the first chapter of the Apocalypse is designed to restore and maintain the confidence of the churches in the utility of their light-bearing function through all time.

Seven golden candlesticks means as many, the whole number that God chooses to use for the purpose. Each candlestick has seven branches—that is, the whole number necessary to make it a complete lamp to light up the place where it is set. The churches of the Lord Jesus Christ in the world are so many candelabra. Every true member is a burner, so that we have just as many lights as we have truly converted souls. The candelabra with which God proposes to light up this dark world are churches of intelligent Christians. Not devotees of a corrupt system, whose policy is to keep the people ignorant in order better to render them manageable by the priesthood. Not languid professors of religion, too indifferent to what is in the Bible to care to know any more of it than that they may feel assured of their own salvation; but men, and women, and children who know the truth, whose minds are full of light, and who do not hide that light—these are the candlesticks. People who know the difference between truth and error, who have risen above old prejudices and ancient superstitions, whose minds are luminous with the great ideas of the Gospel, in whom the Bible is the holy oil which keeps the flame of love and zeal burning, and which makes the sphere of their influence too bright a region for any foolish error or dark sin to be able to hide in—these are the lamps by means of which God proposes to illuminate the earth. As we look at them and remember how many there are of them, how many more than when this vision was beheld by John in Patmos, and how much of earth is now light which was dark then, I am sure our confidence must grow that the whole of what the vision promised is really to come to pass.

Mr. Moody gives an incident from his early experience which is exceedingly suggestive and encouraging.

In his Gospel fishing he had accepted an invitation from a saloon-keeper to hold a meeting in his saloon, on the hard condition of allowing forty-five minutes to the adversaries of Christianity, and then taking but fifteen minutes himself. He commenced with a prayer, at the close of which he was taunted with the fact that the Bible required that two should be "agreed" in praying, for prayer to be answered. But now there knelt at Moody's side a little lad, a child who had been converted in the mission school. As his childish voice rose upon the air it attracted close attention. As he pleaded with the Lord for these wicked men, that the Holy Spirit might show them their error, a great solemnity came upon those hard-hearted infidels and scoffers, and some of them were moved to tears. A sudden panic cleared the room of all but the serious, and the saloon-keeper's children were captured for the Sunday-school, while their father was soon begging Christians to pray for his miserable soul. Could we have a more forcible illustration of the enlightenment possible through one of the youngest and least of God's children? One is reminded of Shakespeare's famous line,

"How far that little candle sends its beams!"

If only a little child, properly taught and under the influence of the Holy Spirit, can shine like that, what will be the result when Sunday-schools, and parental training, and Gospel preaching, and the wide distribution of Bible knowledge have lit up all the golden candlesticks of all the churches?

And then there are *the stars*—that is to say, the

brighter lights of the churches, distinguishable from the churches as stars of the first magnitude are distinguishable from the Milky Way, and as "one star differeth from another star in glory." Great perplexity has arisen from the term "angels," by which the stars are defined; needlessly, it would seem, if it had only been kept in mind that this term belongs to the ideal side of the Church of Christ, the same side to which the term "candlestick" belongs. If the commonplace-looking company of men and women which we call a church, when considered with reference to its possession of divine truth, and its capacity for imparting that truth, deserves to be regarded as a magnificent spiritual candelabrum, then perhaps a man who is the pastor or teacher of this church may properly be called an angel.

We shall not make a serious mistake, I am sure, if we decide to regard the pastor of each church as the angel of the vision. The pastor is the chief teacher of the church, the elder who is to be counted worthy of double honor because, in addition to his ruling, he "labors in the word and doctrine." It is not strange that in the celestial view of such an officer he should be regarded as an angel. What are the angels but "*ministering* spirits sent forth to minister for them who shall be heirs of salvation"? These, too, are *ministers*, commonly designated as such according to our Lord's own instruction, "Whosoever will be great among you, let him be your *minister*"! There really is no such mystery about a minister of the Gospel's being called an angel as is implied by the discussions of the passage. The minister is, on earth, what an angel is in heaven. His work and his spirit are essentially the same, as Doddridge thought when he wrote the hymn which contains the verse,

> " 'Tis not a cause of small import
> The pastor's care demands ;
> But what might fill an *angel's* heart,
> And filled a Saviour's hands."

But it seems to me that, with the pastor, we may place among the "stars" of the churches all who take a prominent part in guiding their thought and moulding their doctrines, all who are pre-eminent in the use of the truth as an instrument for the conversion of sinners and the building up of saints. There is really no sufficient line of demarcation which can be drawn between ministers and teachers who are pastors of churches and those who are evangelists, editors of religious newspapers, authors of good books, professors in Christian colleges and theological seminaries, and all the rest of that numerous class. Of all these alike it may be expected that, being "wise," they shall "shine as the brightness of the firmament," and having "turned many to righteousness," they shall shine "*as the stars* forever and ever." Surely all these deserve to be called stars. And being such, they share with the pastor that weight of responsibility which is laid upon each of the angels to the seven churches, when he is held so largely accountable for the spiritual condition of his church. That condition depends in great measure upon the spiritual food supplied to the Church by its religious guides, and in this feeding of the sheep all who occupy the office of a teacher in any way share. There is, then, no reason for appropriating the term "angel" or that of "star" to the pastor alone; there is every reason for applying both terms to all whose Christian light is specially distinguishable from that of the mass of disciples.

So interpreted, what a perfect constellation—nay, what constellations and galaxies of spiritual stars blaze upon us from out this splendid vision!—as innumerable as those to which God pointed when He desired to strengthen the faith of Abram in his future seed. Thus we may point, in confirmation of our conviction that God means to light up the world with the knowledge of the Gospel. Only to look at these stars, of every magnitude and every variety of color and of beauty, is to gather hope and assurance regarding the grand result of their shining. Think how many more of them there are than there used to be, and how much more brightly they shine! The old stars still shine on with undimmed brilliancy; Origen, and Jerome, and Chrysostom, and Augustine, and Luther, and Calvin, and the rest of the worthies whom time fails to tell of; not one star has fallen nor one beam been quenched. Then think of those which have been added in our own generation, whose lustre appears greater, in some respects, than that of former servants of God. When before was there ever a star like Spurgeon, with his great church and preacher's college, and power to reach the world through the press? Think of Moody, the man who went to England for ten thousand souls, and got them as the seals of his ministry! Think of the churches and schools which he has been the means of establishing! Is there an influence upon earth more royally wide than his? If we stop here with the mention of particular persons, it is only because the number of persons who might be mentioned, on account of their widespread religious influence, is so great as to seem innumerable. How many stars there are! And shall the Church that possesses them, and is destined to possess them in ever-increasing numbers, despair of ever fully illuminating the dark places of the world? On the contrary, the Church must continually increase in confidence that this mighty undertaking is to be thoroughly accomplished, as it beholds with joy the very agents by which the work is to be done.

And yet we have said nothing about *the Sun!* Probability has increased almost to certainty, and yet the great luminary of the Church remains to be considered. What are stars compared with the sun, the great, glorious, almighty sun, "which rejoiceth as a strong man to run its race"? How the beam of even Sirius pales before the first and faintest flashes of the king of day! And the Church has not only seven golden candlesticks, not only seven stars; it has also the Sun of the spiritual world to shed its invincible brilliancy upon the darkness of this. Can there be any doubt of the result? When the Sun of righteousness arises with healing in His wings, what darkness of man or demon can stand before him? Behold a demonstration! The vision which John saw in Patmos is the pledge of the complete enlightenment of the human race.

The sun of this vision is to be considered together with the statement of Jesus Himself in the epilogue of the book, that He is "the bright and morning star." At the date of the giving of this prophecy Jesus could still call Himself by that appellation. He Himself regarded His first advent—nay, the first hundred years of the Christian era, only as the faint morning star which heralded His dispensation. And yet in the first vision of the Apocalypse He shows Himself as the great spiritual Sun of the universe. What is this but the promise of increase of light, until what the world enjoys becomes as much more than the first century saw as the noonday sun exceeds the morning star? The sun is not always to appear only a star. It is destined to come nearer and become brighter, until what seemed, in its far distance, only a tiny point of light, has become a blazing orb, from whose intense heat and light nothing can be hid. The second advent will be to the first advent what a tropical noon is to the faint dawn which has just begun to drive the darkness before it. The history of Christianity, like "the path of the just," is "as a shining light, which shineth more and more unto the perfect day."

Why, every morning that dawns upon the world is a prophecy of the ultimate victory of truth and knowledge over ignorance and error. Not more powerful surely is the natural sun to banish all the darkness of the night than Jesus Christ, the spiritual Sun, the infinite, omniscient God, to overcome the moral darkness of our race. This is the God who is "light," infinite light, and "in Him is no darkness at all." Will the dark places be able to remain dark? Will the shadows and the gloom be able to lurk in the hollows of the earth, when the infinite Sun takes His place in the zenith of the human mind? No, no; it is impossible. This dark earth is to be lit up until it is all bright with Christian knowledge.

Every country road at the autumnal season predicts it. I never see the mullein stalks, with their tips of yellow bloom, but I think of a lighted candle. The mulleins stand all along the wayside, and the goldenrods all aflame, to tell how God will yet light up the world with His seven golden candlesticks. The progress of artificial illumination is a token of the same kind. The streets of towns and cities which were once dangerously dark at night are now delightfully irradiated with the moonlight of electricity. What does it all mean, but that moral and spiritual darkness is to be driven away by the light of revealed truth and Christian knowledge? "The night is far spent; the day is at hand." "Weeping may endure for a night, but joy cometh in the morning." When the morning comes it will be a great satisfaction to be able to feel that we helped to bring it forward.

IV.

THE EPISTLES TO THE SEVEN CHURCHES.

If we have really found the missing key, and correctly conceived the purpose of the Apocalypse, the great prophecy which it contains is that this dark world of ours is to be lighted up with truth, until all error shall have been dispelled and sin shall have been rendered impossible. We are now to see whether the first section of the book, containing the epistles to the seven churches, can be harmonized with this idea, and get a rational interpretation from it.

What could be more natural, or indeed more necessary, at this point, than a divine assurance that the extraordinary plan already announced has been conceived and is entertained in entire soberness of spirit, and with a clear perception of all the discouraging facts in the actual situation? The world to be lighted up with truth? All minds to be imbued with knowledge? The superstitions, and mistakes, and deceptions of the entire human race to be banished forever from the earth by the universal prevalence of Christian ideas? The thought is yet overwhelming! The possibility seems in the highest degree improbable. Such a state of things appears the most impossible of dreams. After eighteen hundred years of Christian progress human ignorance is still so dense, and error so firmly intrenched in the minds of men, that anything like general enlightenment seems indefinitely far away. Is it possible that the Bible actually pledges itself to such a revolution? Can it be that Inspiration authorizes us to expect such an immense and glorious reversal of the present situation?

Yes, it is there in the introduction of this last book of the Bible. This is the last word of comfort which Inspiration has to utter, and it is, indeed, a great word. Be not appalled at the thought of the deep darkness which enshrouds the human mind! Do not despond because the world can never be truly and generally Christian until it is generally enlightened! It is to be enlightened; God has decreed it; He has not only decreed it, but He has already provided the means by which the illumination is to be effected. Behold the lamps which are to light up the dark places! Seven candlesticks, seven stars, the Sun! So much we learn from the first chapter of the Apocalypse.

But it is as if we had entered an aerial ship and been lifted to an altitude which makes us dizzy. What more natural than alarm at such an experience? Can we trust our pilot? Does he know what he is about? Is Inspiration here as elsewhere the same wise and steady guide? Are these magnificent ideas, is this sublime and glorious conception of the world's future, framed in sober knowledge of present discouraging facts, and all the tremendous difficulties which such a plan must meet with? The sun? Yes, the sun is infinite in its resources, and the stars seem comparatively unlimited in their power to shine; but what about the candlesticks? Does the Author of this plan expect much from them? Does He understand the feebleness of these light-bearers? Let us have, before we proceed further in this alarming voyage, something to steady our mental nerves and assure us of sober and safe guidance!

Accordingly just at this point, before we are carried still higher into the symbolic glories of the heavenly state, the divine Inspirer of this wonderful book pauses to give us the desired assurance. Parting the curtains of our chariot of fire He points downward to the earth, and bids us perceive that He has made no mistake as to the actual situation. Look, He says; yonder is the world, just as it is, in all its ignorance, folly, and sin. I do not overlook a single impediment to this proposed transformation. There are the seven churches. I see them just as they are. All their imperfections are entirely plain to My mind. I know just what they are and what can be done with them. Reassure yourselves as to My perfect comprehension of all the elements of this problem, and trust Me, in all the surprising revelations that I shall give you, to speak always without extravagance and without misconception!

The epistles to the seven churches are precisely such a combination of the exalted imagery which fills the book with the prosaic language of common sense and practical knowledge, as to produce the calming and reassuring effect which I have described. The symbolism is not dropped, or rather it is dropped, but only for a moment at a time. Each epistle begins and closes with something of the same splendid imagery to which we have been introduced in the first chapter.

We are not permitted to forget that our chariot is a celestial one, or to get out of it. The vision of the Son of man, with His face like the sun, holding the seven stars in His right hand and surrounded by the seven golden candlesticks, continues before our eyes. But we are permitted to look down from the chariot upon the earth below, while our conductor describes the scene. We recognize the entire correctness of his description, and see that he has not omitted one shadow or exaggerated or misrepresented one unimportant particular.

In the epistles to the seven churches, their ideal character, as candlesticks, to illuminate the world's darkness, is suggested in each introduction and implied in each conclusion. A striking part of this ideal representation is the calling the pastor or teacher of each church by the celestial title of angel. As a golden candlestick the church is seen associated with the great spiritual Sun and with the angelic stars; that is the ideal side of the representation.

But between the introduction and the conclusion of each epistle is a plain, unvarnished statement of the actual spiritual condition of the church addressed. These statements are so clear-sighted in their perception of faults and evils, so true to what we know of actual church life, that we recognize their truthfulness to facts even the most discouraging. We perceive that, however splendid these representative churches are in their ideal character, in their real character they are thoroughly understood.

At the beginning of each address the divine Correspondent says, "*I know.*" And what does He know?

That Ephesus has cooled in its affection; that Smyrna is poor; that Pergamos is hard by the throne of Satan; that Thyatira is heretical; that Sardis is dead; that Philadelphia is opposed by Satan's synagogue, and that Laodicea is lukewarm. Surely this is no extravagant estimate of the Church and its attainments. These calm and even sad admissions of the faults and errors of the early churches may at once and finally deliver us from the fear that the promises and predictions of the Apocalypse, extraordinary as they are, are founded in any weak partiality to the churches or blindness to their deficiencies. The rapt vision of our prophetic guide sees the facts of earth in all their repulsiveness and all their difficulty. He knows just how dark the darkness is which He proposes to remove, and He is quite aware how much of that darkness yet abides in the very lamps which He proposes to use.

Nevertheless He does not despond. In full sight of all the difficulties, He does not abate one jot of His confidence that the desired result is to be attained. This is the fact that encourages us and raises our hopes to the height necessary to the full enjoyment of the prophecy. Our Lord sees the great and alarming faults of the churches, and yet He does not despair of them. He even contemplates the possibility that some may lose all power to give light, and cease to be candlesticks at all. Yet He does not give up His plan to light up the world, and expects to have candlesticks enough to accomplish His purpose.

Meanwhile, in these same epistles our Lord proceeds to trim His lamps. If one examine the seven letters critically, as to what is the chief burden of their teachings, he will acknowledge that they relate principally to purity of doctrine and faithfulness in testimony. How did the Master expect these churches to accomplish their mission? How were they to let their light shine? First, and chiefly, by carefulness regarding the correctness of the doctrine held and taught by them. Ephesus is commended for having successfully endured a trial of its orthodoxy; Smyrna, for resisting the blasphemies of a false Judaism; Pergamos, for not having denied the faith; Philadelphia, for keeping Christ's Word. Blame is visited upon Pergamos and Thyatira for holding false doctrine and suffering it to be taught. Sardis is admonished to remember how it has received and heard, and to hold fast and repent. The reader must be left to make his own examination in order to see how largely the correctness of the creeds of these churches is the burden of the epistles to them. It is exactly what it should be if these letters were designed to stimulate the churches to efficiency as the light-bearers of the world, and if the first condition of that efficiency be correct Gospel ideas.

In this age, when so much is said of the unimportance of *theology* as compared with *religion*, it will do us good to recur to the epistles to the seven churches. These are the last recorded communications of our ascended Lord to His people upon earth. What does He say to them? What does He urge upon them as of the most vital importance? Does He say, Be active and enterprising, be consistent and holy, be inventive and aggressive in capturing the world for Me?

No, there is not much about these matters in these epistles. They are essential, no doubt, and elsewhere the Master has instructed us regarding them. But in these final communications His admonition is, Be wise! Know the truth! Understand the great Gospel ideas! For if we know the truth, and hold it without prejudice or misconception, that truth will make us free from all bondage to sin; it will create in us everything that is good, and cause us to light up our corner of the earth so brightly that no badness can continue to dwell there. Everything else depends upon the possession of "the truth as it is in Jesus."

There is perhaps no portion of the Word of God which must bear a severer criticism than these same epistles. Their claims are such as can be sustained only by the loftiest conceivable character; for they assume to be the epistles not of Paul, or Peter, or John, but of Jesus Christ Himself, and of Him not in His state of earthly humiliation, but in that of His heavenly glory.

If the Apocalypse were regarded as a fiction, how hard it would have been to have invented this portion of it! The medium who pretends to have received a communication from some departed statesman, generally perpetrates some solecism which stamps the production as a forgery. How hard it is to produce a letter from the other world worthy to be attributed to Webster, or Lincoln, or Washington! But these epistles claim to be dictated by the glorified Saviour. The utmost pains is taken to heighten our sense of the grandeur of their origin. They are from the great Sun of the spiritual universe, from Him who holds the star-like intelligences in His right hand, from the Author of the Bible, from the Sender of the Holy Spirit, from the awful I Am, who is the same yesterday, to-day, and forever. It is the highest possible praise to be able to say that these epistles seem worthy of their origin. They approve themselves as fit to have proceeded from the glorified Christ. The influence of their worth extends beyond themselves, and sheds confidence upon the whole of the strange book in which they are found imbedded. From the value of that portion of which we are so much more capable of judging we justly infer the value of all the rest, even while it remains incomprehensible to us.

The son of John Albert Bengel, the author of the Gnomon on the New Testament, has added a note to that commentary containing his honored father's tribute to the seven epistles when near his end. "I remember," says the son, "that, just at the last hours of his pilgrimage (1752), my sainted parent earnestly commended to his family the frequent reading and study of the epistles in the Apocalypse, adding as the reason, 'There is scarce anything that can press to the depths of one's nature with such purifying power.'" Bengel was a qualified judge, whose opinion is of the utmost weight. But he is only one of many who have felt and owned the purifying power of these celestial communications. As we read them it is easy to see our Saviour in the very act of trimming the lamps of the churches that they may shed a clearer light.

The demand upon these seven epistles is nothing less than that they should be such as to serve as the substantial foundation of the whole series of sublime visions which make up the Apocalypse. These visions rise, like Pelion upon Ossa, in continually growing splendor and glory, until their top reaches heaven, and is clothed with the magnificence of eternity. For such a prophetic work no common foundation would have sufficed. It must be broad enough and firm enough to sustain all the weight of the immense fabric resting upon it, without a suspicion of a tremor. That is precisely what these epistles are. There is nothing in the subsequent visions, however wonderful, which is not implied by something in these. All that is afterward said with such efflorescence of imagination is warranted by something in the epistles. Here, where the Lord Christ is speaking in the calm, clear language of common sense and every-day life, where, in His description of facts, He is exact and even prosaic, He yet promises all and foresees all that, when afterward expanded, seems so extraordinary. Here as well as there His purpose to light up the world is calmly asserted, and He hesitates not to anticipate all the sublime consequences of that great act. Here as well as there the New Jerusalem is seen coming down from God out of heaven in all the effulgence of the latter-day glory. Distinctly perceiving all that is lacking in His Church, perceiving all its wrong tendencies and mistakes and sins, He yet speaks with entire confidence of the future. What more could we have? There is a great task before the Church; to man it seems impossible to illuminate the world with truth; but having talked with our Lord about it in these lower altitudes, and heard Him speak with such divine assurance of the result to be accomplished, we may now fearlessly ascend into the upper regions of the prophecy, knowing that there, as here, all is guaranteed by reality.

In that grand drama to which the apostle now introduces us, where the surprises of human invention are so outdone by the inspired imagination as to seem tame and poor; surrounded by beings stranger than eye ever saw, and by falling stars, and flying angels, and heavenly thrones, and a dissolving and reconstructed universe, we will not doubt that every scene is contrived with wisdom, and reveals substantial truth. We will echo the answer of the child who was asked if he would fear to ride in a chariot like Elijah's? "No," he replied, "not if God drove." The epistles to the seven churches have accomplished their chief purpose when they have satisfied us that God Himself is to be our guide through all the marvels and prodigies of the remainder of the book to a not doubtful termination, and that that termination is to be the entire conquest of the error of earth by the almightiness of truth.

V.

HEAVEN THE SOURCE OF LIGHT.

AND now farewell to fear, farewell to earth; upward and onward be our course under the guidance of our celestial Pilot, until our eyes behold the city of God, the central metropolis of the universe. For where else should we go? The question whether earth can ever be lighted up with heavenly wisdom depends upon how great that heavenly wisdom is. If there be enough of it earth can be illuminated. The first question, then, to have answered, is the old question of human perplexity, "Is there knowledge with the Most High?" And the second question is, How can that knowledge be communicated to men? The first act of the prophetic drama is devoted to answering these two questions.

How natural and necessary the descriptions which now follow, upon the theory that the lighting up of the world with truth is the subject of the Apocalypse! Having announced this grand subject in the first chapter, and shown in the second and third chapters that this sublime conception is entertained in sober acquaintance with all that might be said against it, the proper action of the prophecy now begins with a vision of heaven. When we have seen what heaven is we shall know what can be done with earth. The important fact for us to notice is that heaven is described with special reference to *its illuminating power*.

First let us observe that the description of God which is given in the fourth chapter is substantially the reappearance of the celestial sun of the first chapter. There we had one like unto the Son of man, with white hair, eyes like unto a flame of fire, feet like burning brass, and countenance, or, as some take it, the whole appearance, "as the sun shineth in his strength." Here He that sits upon the throne is "like a jasper and a sardine stone, with a rainbow round about the throne." The difference between the two representations we may consider to be due to the difference of situations of the beholder. The fiery splendor of the Sun of righteousness, which blinds and kills any mortal spectator, the glorified can look upon without pain or injury. To them that splendor is tempered and softened, so that they can see God and not die. We are now in vision with John in heaven, and can therefore look upon the God of light as we look upon one of earth's flashing gems. But with this difference of softness produced by proximity, the identity of the divine appearances in the two visions is unmistakable.

Imagine a gigantic jasper and sardine stone of human or greater dimensions, and think what its appearance would be! Alford says that it would be "white light mingled with fire." What is that but the sun? That it is the sun, the "rainbow round about the throne" is the emphatic and sufficient witness. The rainbow is the child of the sunshine and the rain — impossible apart from the bright rays of the solar light. What is betokened by the predominance in the bow of the emerald tint we may not now stop to conjecture; but the bow itself is the reminder of God's covenant with earth not again to destroy it, and may, indeed, remind us of His "new and better covenant" and of His abundant ability to fulfil His promises, especially this mighty promise of the enlightenment of the world.

Observe also that whereas, in the first vision, the Son of man held seven stars in His right hand, here "seven lamps of fire burn before the throne," explained to be the "seven spirits of God." Again, perhaps nearness accounts for softness of radiance and clearness of outline. What at a distance appears a flashing point, a star on the horizon, when approached proves to be a lamp in some cottage window. We are not obliged to identify the "seven lamps of fire" with the seven angelic stars. For as the light that is in all created beings is only derived and not original, it is a matter of course that when we trace the light of any spiritual star, human or angelic, to its source, we shall find it to be the illuminating power of God's Holy Spirit.

Thus have been indicated the wisdom and knowledge of God, who is the source of all truth and the fountain of all knowledge throughout the universe. Next we have the knowledge and wisdom *of the Church* represented by the twenty-four elders crowned and enthroned close about the throne of central Deity. Twelve of these elders represent the Jewish Church, twelve the Christian Church. They suggest to us the matured and sanctified wisdom of patriarchs and apostles after all the centuries of experience and culture which these worthies have enjoyed. What men Abraham, and Moses, and Daniel, and Paul, and John were two thousand to four thousand years ago! What men they must be by this time, after such an extended period of growth and improvement! What a congress of sanctified human intellect gathers in the eternal world, into which the riches of earth are continually pouring! If that congress deliberates upon earthly affairs, what profound sagacity, what broad statesmanship, what lofty conceptions, what far-reaching foresight those deliberations must reveal!

It would be more than we know to say that our great struggle here is directly assisted by the wisdom of the former leaders of the Church. It must be taken as the symbol and suggestion of the growing wisdom of the Church on earth. To us who have the garnered results of what God said " to the fathers by the prophets," and to whom He " hath in these last days spoken by His Son," is not the transmitted and accumulated knowledge of the earthly Church worthy to be represented by those constellations of glorified intelligence whom we contemplate as dwelling now in the heavens?

Then there are the four living creatures about whom there have been endless disputes into which it is not necessary to enter. So much as this is certainly clear, that they stand for the aggregate of *created intelligence*. Error can hope to maintain itself only through the absence of the powers of observation and understanding. Against error and for truth is the fact of intelligence in all its forms, in all places, ever studying, ever finding out that of which it has been ignorant, ever gathering knowledge of new facts, and so making the knowledge of other facts possible. It is the symbolic expression of this general intelligence which I find in the four living creatures. They are composites of all classes of animal forms. They have eyes—in fact, are "*full of eyes*" within and without, which is the most impressive part of the description of them.

If we turn to the fuller description in the prophecy of Ezekiel, where undoubtedly the same symbols occur, we come upon language which makes these living creatures seem still fitter to belong to a picture of heavenly knowledge. "Their appearance was like *burning coals of fire*, and like the appearance of *lamps*, and the *fire was bright*, and out of the fire went forth *lightning.*" "And the living creatures ran, and returned as the appearance of a *flash of lightning.*" Think how a flash of lightning in the darkest night makes all objects suddenly and plainly visible, and you perceive that John was not the first to be inspired to use these symbols of illumination. The later Scripture takes for granted the knowledge of the earlier Scripture. But now that we have supplied it, and can see these four living creatures not only as full of eyes within and without, but also as glowing with the brightness of lamps of fire and the almost insufferable splendor of burning coals of fire and even of the lightning flash, is it not evident that we are looking upon a vision precisely of the same kind with the opening vision of the Apocalypse?

I have, then, justified my assertion that the vision

of heaven in the fourth chapter of this book is substantially a renewal of the vision of the Son of man in the first chapter. Its special teaching is the power of heaven to illuminate dark places. The divine King, "like unto a jasper and sardine stone"—*i.e.*, "white light mingled with fire," creating a rainbow by His effulgence; the seven lamps or torches burning before the throne, the secret sources of the light of the seven stars, and these living creatures full of eyes like burning coals and lamps and lightning—what is this but the picture of the fact that heaven is just that place of lamps, just that fountain of light and truth, which earth's darkness needs? As we see what heaven is, we know what earth must become.

And now, in the fifth chapter, we have a dramatic action designed to answer the question, How shall heaven's knowledge displace earth's ignorance? It is almost startling to find the answer so exactly in accordance with the theory which we have undertaken to test by applying it to the various parts of the Apocalypse. For the answer is *a book*—a book resting upon the hand of its divine Author. A book is the very means by which one of us human beings attempts to give the information which he possesses to his fellow-creatures. A book means, and can only mean, the publication to the world of the knowledge which God alone originally has. It is by a book—the Bible —that God has already sought to remove human ignorance. Nature itself—the older revelation—may be regarded as an open volume for human instruction. This is God's method to subjugate to Himself the world, to let the light of His truth shine into human hearts until it shall have become impossible not to love and serve Him. "*In Thy light shall we see light.*" This has always been God's plan. Here in the Revelation we find God's last word upon His plan, and we find Him adhering to and not departing from His plan from the beginning.

There have been many guesses as to the nature and contents of this book seen by John in or upon the divine hand. Some think it to be the Apocalypse itself, some the book of destiny, some the book of God's judgments. My theory requires that it should be *all the additional light* necessary to the conversion of mankind. Not necessarily a new revelation; perhaps chiefly light upon the old revelations, the light which God has and always has had, but which we yet lack. God, we must remember, has always been in possession of the facts which would have made rebellion and unbelief impossible. If mankind had always known what God has always known our human career of impiety could hardly have taken place. What is needed to check that career, always including the work of the Holy Spirit upon the heart, is for the divine knowledge to become human knowledge. More and more light must shine. The progress of discovery, which is only the other side of the progress of revelation, must put beyond question truths now debated. The inspiration of the Bible, the divinity of our Lord, and the virtue of His atonement must cease to be debatable questions. The time must come when men can no longer any more doubt what are the facts about God, or sin, or salvation, than they can deny gravitation or the Copernican system. This era of light will be to our present situation what noonday is to the dawn. And all the difference between present knowledge and that full and overwhelming knowledge may be considered as the contents of that book which John saw upon the hand of its divine Author.

This view of the book makes intelligible the grief of John at the apparent impossibility of having it unsealed and read. "I wept much," he says, "because no one was found worthy to open the book or to look thereon." This grief is hardly comprehensible upon the supposition that it was the book of destiny, or of judgments, or the Apocalypse itself. But if it was the book of divine knowledge which needed to become human knowledge in order for this world to become the kingdom of heaven, no wonder that John wept when it seemed as if the book could not possibly be opened.

Nothing could be truer to the facts than the description. The book, complete and ready, resting upon the hand of the Author, sets forth the disposition of God to enlighten mankind. But there are certain difficulties, apparently great and insuperable difficulties, about the reception of this enlightenment by men. These difficulties, and not any objections originating with God, it seems to me must be what is represented by the seven seals. There are difficulties enough to account for the seals without supposing that God arbitrarily or voluntarily adds to their number. It is true, terribly true, that man has it in his power to obstruct the progress of the knowledge of God. God makes books; men put seals upon them. And the question of questions is—no wonder that John wept at the prospect of its being negatived—whether those seals can be broken, whether the impediments to the spiritual education of the human race can be overcome, whether the locks which confine the human mind in its dungeon of darkness can be removed. These seals we can see ; it requires no high power of imagination to conceive what they can be ; they look so massive and mighty that we despair of their removal, and it is unnecessary to spend our thought upon divine objections to human education, when human objections and obstructions are so plain and palpable.

As a matter of fact, the progress of the human mind in the acquisition of divine knowledge is possible only by a succession of victories. A second step toward truth becomes practicable because a previous step has been gained. Not till that preparatory step has been taken is the way open to take the next step. The world waited for a proper interpretation of the first chapter of Genesis until the lately born science of geology made that interpretation possible. Ignorance of that science was, up to the time of its inception, a seal which locked up the meaning of the truth. In like manner ignorance of any class of facts is a bar to the understanding of some other facts, a seal upon the divine book of knowledge which effectually restrains study until the seal is broken. In order to understand all things which it is needful to know, the last seal must disappear which some special ignorance imposes. When all studies have reached their results and all discoveries have been made in all departments of research, the light of general and sufficient information will shine into all minds, and men, the men that can be saved by light, will everywhere know too much to be able to continue in folly and rebellion.

Is the breaking of the seals, then, a wholly human process of investigation and acquisition ? By no means. The human faculties have their appointed place in the work, but it is God that worketh all in all. The providence of the divine mind is nowhere more marked than in the advancement of true learning. Discovery follows discovery, truth follows truth, not only because man searches and finds, but because God guides and reveals.

The greatest secret of the intellectual success of the race is the revealing power of Christianity. This is the rational interpretation of the ascription of worthiness to the Lamb uttered by the representatives of the glorified Church in this vision. They cry, "Thou art worthy to take the book, and to open the seals thereof: for *Thou wast slain*, and hast *redeemed us* unto God *by Thy blood* out of every kindred, and tongue, and people, and nation ; and hast made us unto our God kings and priests : and we shall reign on the earth." There throbs through this ascription of praise the living consciousness of the saved soul that the death of Christ was the birth of a new humanity and the pledge of a regenerated world.

Each child of God who understands his own spiritual life knows that it was the sight of the Cross which the Holy Spirit used when Christ first became to him *wisdom*. It was the power of the preaching of the Cross by which, as a means, God, who commanded the light to shine out of darkness, shined in his heart to give the light of the knowledge of the glory of God in the face of Jesus Christ. It is from the live coals on the altar where Christ was offered as a sacrifice for sin that each Christian lights that torch which henceforth throws its light upon everything which he considers. No wonder that the saved disciple has such faith in that which has illuminated him. Why should he not expect that the Lamb slain from the foundation of the world may be to unnumbered others what He has been to him, and that the radiance of Calvary is to extend to the utmost limits of the race? The Crucifixion is the key-fact of human history. Christ crucified opens the doors of all knowledge. If it had not been for His death, the story of the human race would have forever continued a hopeless puzzle. Since that so much has become intelligible that it may be hoped that all will be. He who has shed so much light may be trusted to shed more light, until all becomes clear. With the Bible for our text-book and the Holy Spirit for our instructor all riddles will be read, and all mysteries which stand in the way of human salvation will finally be explained.

VI.

THE OPENING OF THE SEVEN SEALS.

If now our conception of the subject of the Apocalypse be correct, and our principle of interpretation the true one, we ought to find in the description of the opening of the seven seals the seven stages of a great progress in the mental illumination of the world. We ought to find depicted the successive steps of a march the goal of which is the complete spiritual enlightenment of mankind. Let me not here or elsewhere be misunderstood. I am not speaking of universal salvation, but of that general prevalence of the knowledge of the Lord which is the indispensable condition of His receiving the "heathen" for His "inheritance," and "the uttermost parts of the earth for" His "possession."

It does not follow, however, that the description is to be a literal one. On the contrary, the very character of the book requires that it should be symbolic. A literal description of the progress of truth consequent upon the removal of the great obstacles which hold it in check would be a prophetic anticipation of the varying course of human opinions, and the victories of revealed truth over the false philosophy, sophistry, and heresy of our race. Such a statement, in advance, of the long and intricate struggle in the realm of thought, we cannot suppose likely to have been given by inspiration. It would have been even more unintelligible to most minds than the symbolism of this book has proved. All that could be done in depicting such a conflict was to set forth, by means of pictures, some general idea of the struggle, and to show it advancing to triumph.

The trouble with many expositors has been that they have seen no way but to take these descriptions literally. These pictures of war, famine, and pestilence, instead of being regarded as shadows of changes in the realm of ideas, have been supposed by many to mean *only* war, famine, and pestilence. Great efforts have been made to identify the particular historical events which, it was supposed, are here singled out for their pre-eminent influence upon the fortunes of the Church. Rival historical interpreters have contended for particular battles, famines, and pestilences which seemed to them to have special claims to attention by the inspired author. It is almost needless to say that no interpretation of this kind has ever established itself as conclusive, or can ever be pronounced more certain than any other.

Another class of interpreters are satisfied to take the phenomena described in a general sense. They are not, however, consistent in adhering to this plan through the whole description, but having taken a part of it to be general, they still consider another part as particular. There is no end to the confusion introduced by such a method of interpretation. Alford, for example, makes the first five seals symbolic expressions of victory, war, famine, pestilence, and martyrdom in general, but insists that the sixth seal belongs to a particular event—the judgment. One result of this method of interpretation is that the end of all things is reached under the sixth seal, leaving the seventh seal to be superfluous.

The person who takes these descriptions literally imposes upon himself the task of explaining what literal war, famine, and pestilence have to do with the progress of Christ's kingdom. Even though he take them generally, he does not escape that necessity. It is no easy task. Not that an ingenious mind might not show that these have resulted in religious progress. God has undoubtedly used war, famine, and pestilence for the furtherance of His cause. But the selection of these classes of events, one for each seal, if they are taken literally, requires that they should be shown to be *more* helpful to Christianity than any other classes of events. Is that true? Can it be proved to be the fact that war, famine, and pestilence have contributed *more* to the advancement of the divine kingdom than peace, plenty, and health? Perhaps it can, but it is difficult; nobody, at any rate, has yet attempted it. To justify a literal interpretation it must be shown that the clash of arms and the horrors of war have had a *principal* place as means of the world's improvement.

For myself I cannot think that these great evils and curses have had, or can have, such a place among God's means of grace. I know that "He maketh the wrath of man to praise Him," but not surely as much as He makes the Gospel of His Son and the brotherly love of His people. He has overruled these things, no doubt, to His glory; they have contributed somewhat, beyond question, by their stern teaching, to human improvement; but to give them the *chief* place in God's scheme, which they seem to have by a literal interpretation of the pictures disclosed by the breaking of the seven seals, is to reverse all our ideas of the divine methods. Besides, we have abundant *warning* against this method of interpretation. Over and over we are admonished that the real fighting intended in the Apocalypse is altogether spiritual. "I will fight against thee with the sword of *My mouth*," says the great Figure of the prophecy to one of His erring churches. It is not material warfare that this book describes, but the inevitable battle, the "irrepressible conflict" of truth with falsehood.

Not expecting now to find a literal description of this conflict, which would be to tell beforehand what all the heresiarchs from Celsus to Ingersoll, or Ingersoll's most distant successor, would have to say, and how the champions of orthodoxy would reply to them; still less expecting to be able to show how the great curses of the world have subserved the purpose of the truth pre-eminently, we come to this question, Are the pictures described in the account of the opening of the seven seals such as to serve as a representation of the progress of light in overcoming the moral darkness of mankind? Does the symbolism admit of being interpreted as the successive steps of that advance which the truth of God must make upon the removal, one after another, of the great impediments which stand in its way? To this it may be replied emphatically, Yes! So looked at, these images fall into order and appear to have a worthy meaning. In this way we find that progress, that harmony, that correlation of thought, which we are warranted in expecting in a divine communication to men.

According to this idea we should anticipate in the first picture the weakest expression of the conception of progress. Expositors have been puzzled by the fact that the conqueror upon a white horse seems the symbol of complete victory. If he be that there is no progress of thought, for what should be the last picture is put first. The end would appear at the opening of the first seal, and the opening of the other six would become unnecessary.

Let me now put before the reader my own conception of the significance of this series of symbols.

The first four seals are represented as disclosing four remarkable horsemen. These horsemen make their appearance at the call of the four living creatures who symbolize created intelligence. These creatures cry "Come!" one after another, as with a voice of thunder, which must signify the strength of the demand for these successive disclosures of the truth. Elsewhere in the Apocalypse thunder is the voice of God, as it is also in the Gospels, especially in that memorable instance where God spoke to the Son, and "the people said it thundered." In this case, then, we have the human demand for more knowledge reinforced by the divine demand; "vox populi" is also "vox Dei."

These living creatures cry "Come!" in a certain order, which is evidently significant of the growing strength of the demand of intelligence for truth. The first living creature was "like a lion;" the second, "like a calf" or ox; the third "had a face as of a man," and the fourth "was like a flying eagle." These forms are certainly not to be regarded as equals in their symbolization of intelligence. The lion, though the king of savage beasts, falls below the humblest of the domestic animals. "The ox knoweth his owner, and the ass his master's crib." Man rises far above the most sagacious of his brute servants. But it is redeemed and regenerated man who, by waiting upon the Lord, "mounts up with wings as eagles," and becomes a partaker of the divine nature. These living creatures, then, who voice the demand of intelligence for increase of light, do so in the order of their degree of intelligence. It is as if, first, the wild beasts cried "Come;" then the domestic animals; then the human race in its natural wisdom, and finally Christian wisdom enlightened and quickened by the Holy Spirit.

A similar progress can be seen in the appearances of the horsemen, who must represent the truth itself in its growth and extension. The first should, of course, represent the first successes of the Gospel. The picture is that of a warrior upon a white horse, with a bow in his hand, whose victories are yet principally anticipatory. His fair array is yet unstained by the gore of actual fighting; he is more like a holiday warrior on dress parade crowned by the good opinions of beholders with the assurance of success. It is a fitting symbol with which to begin a series which is to go on increasing in signs of power to the last of the series.

The second picture, by common consent, stands for

war, real and sanguinary. It is a rider upon a *red* horse, whose battles have stained him with blood, who has power to take peace from the earth, and whose weapon is not a bow, but a sword ; not the instrument of distant attack, but of hand-to-hand fighting. Here is progress such as our minds demand from the latent power indicated by the appearance of resources, to the actual power exercised by disciplined and veteran valor.

The third seal being opened, we see a rider upon a *black* horse, who has a balance in his hands, and is the awful emblem of famine. Of war and famine, which is the stronger idea? Famine undoubtedly ; where war slays its thousands, famine slays its ten thousands. The besieged city endures all assaults but that of starvation. Jerusalem was conquered not by the soldiers of Titus, but by that awful destitution of food which made a mother kill, and cook, and devour her own child.

It must be said, however, that the figure is not intended to be understood in this extremity of its greatness. It is not utter famine that is to be thought of, where there is nothing whatever to eat, but only that moderate stringency where food is scarce and comparatively high priced. Even such a degree of deprivation is more dreadful to a nation than war. Even at such a time there will be distress in many quarters, like that in Ireland when that pathetic poem was written,

"Give me three grains of corn, mother,
Give me three grains of corn !"

And now, what is stronger than famine ? Death

upon his *pale* horse, whom the opening of the fourth seal discloses. Famine slays many, but death slays all. Of all these terrible riders upon horses, Death is the most terrible. He is a conqueror who lays all lives low.

It is obvious that we have reached a limit in this direction. This quaternion of cavalry exhausts the possibilities of this kind of imagery, and the varieties of earthly intelligence which call for progress are also exhausted. An uninspired imagination might have faltered here, unable to find an image which should still further heighten the idea of the growing power of truth upon the removal of successive obstacles to its progress. We have been told that it is like a warrior upon a white horse before the battle, exultant with the confidence of victory; like a battle-scarred warrior upon a red horse, slaying his thousands; like Famine, slaying his tens of thousands; and finally like Death, slaying all. How can the idea of power in conquest be carried still further?

By passing into the world of the dead, and picturing the intermediate state. And now the power portrayed is no longer mere brute force, but moral power. It is moral power exerted through *prayer*, in circumstances precisely such as to make prayer most overwhelmingly powerful. It is the souls of the martyrs who pray, and they call upon God for justice, only for justice; and how can a good God refuse to heed such a prayer? The thought is inconceivable, so that we have risen to a conception of the power of prayer when it is omnipotent.

But here for the first time the symbolism is of such

a kind as to suggest the real nature of the conflict and of the successes gained. The four previous seals are represented as being opened in sympathy with the desire of the fourfold intelligence of the world for the coming of a better kingdom. But the breaking of the fifth seal reveals the desire of a still higher intelligence. It is that of martyr spirits, who have added to their Christian knowledge in this life the acquisitions of the intermediate state. If the knowledge which shall prevail in the earth upon the removal of the fifth great obstacle to enlightenment be worthy to be represented by that of sanctified souls in the intermediate state, what knowledge that will be!

Perhaps it is intended to suggest to us an age when the crimes of the martyr ages will at length appear to mankind in their true light, and the long-sleeping sense of justice toward the Church of the Lord Jesus Christ will awaken everywhere through the world. That time cannot yet be said to have arrived, for though persecution of the early sort has generally ceased, it still remains true that they that "will be godly must suffer persecution." There are not wanting signs, however, that the "good time coming" is on the way, when the Church, instead of being maligned and opposed, shall everywhere be honored and assisted.

The sixth seal is now opened, and the picture chosen to illustrate the knowledge of the period for which this seal stands is the description of the Judgment Day. Alford and others are not wrong in saying that the language is that elsewhere used to depict the end of the world. They are wrong, however, in taking the language historically as a prophetic announcement of the second and personal coming of Christ. So understood, there would be nothing more for a seventh seal to introduce, because the coming which is the subject of the book (according to that interpretation) would have taken place. But according to the view here taken, the coming is that of Christ *in the truth*, and to set it forth the judgment scene is here used not historically, but only symbolically.

As a symbol of the progress of knowledge, the Judgment is in advance of the intermediate state. The intermediate state is in advance of all knowledge in this life, but the Judgment is in advance of the intermediate state, because it is the end of that state. At the Judgment all will be known that needed to be known in order to pass the final sentence upon all souls. In accordance with this fact, the knowledge here expressed is attributed not to the holy martyrs, but to the great sinners of the world. The progress of enlightenment seems now to have gone so far that not only the good, but the bad understand; not only the pure in heart see God, but the leaders of human wickedness, no longer able to be blind to their situation, see it so clearly as to cry to the mountains and the rocks to fall upon them and to "hide them from the face of Him that sitteth upon the throne, and from the wrath of the Lamb." If this blazing brightness of the Judgment Day is to be taken symbolically of a period of human history, what a period of general and clear acknowledgment of truths long denied and resisted it will be!

Dr. Justin A. Smith, whose valuable authority I am glad to be able to quote for the opinion that the scenes of the Judgment Day are used in this place symbolically, also agrees with me so far as to infer that the symbolism implies changes upon earth of the greatest magnitude. "Doubtless," he says, "it can be only great and awful events which may appropriately be represented under such imagery; revolutions wide-reaching and overwhelming, a downfall of earthly powers and dignities as great as the imagination is capable of conceiving." The difference between Dr. Smith and myself relates chiefly to the nature of these remarkable changes. He has in mind political revolutions, which I am far from denying may be included; but my main idea is of revolutions in the region of ideas. "Ideas," says Bishop Vincent, "are the factors that lift civilization. They create revolutions. There is more dynamite in an idea than in many bombs." In accordance with the thought thus so happily expressed, I would say that a state of society worthy to be symbolized by the scenes of the Judgment Day must be one in which the whole intellectual and moral foundations, as at present existing, shall have been utterly exploded and tumbled into ruins. Must it not eventually be so? Must not the time come when the selfish and worldly principles on which mankind at large base their lives shall be quite superseded by the principles of the Gospel of Christ? When that time comes "the kings of the earth, and the princes, and the military tribunes, and the rich, and the strong, and every bond man, and free man" will have to get out of the world or join the glorious company of those whose practice agrees with the acknowledged principles of a true life.

THE OPENING OF THE SEVEN SEALS. 73

And now have we not reached the end ? Can symbolism go any further ? What remains to stand for that period which shall succeed the removal of the last great obstacle to human enlightenment, the obstacle represented by the seventh seal ? Why, the picture of *heaven.* The rider upon the white horse, upon the red horse, upon the black horse, upon the pale horse, the intermediate state, and the Judgment Day are a series of sublime symbols which require but one idea more to complete them—that of heaven.

Accordingly in the seventh chapter of the Apocalypse we find ourselves once more in the heaven described at the beginning of this vision. Once more we are in the presence of the throne, and of the elders, and of the four living creatures. But now the saved are here with the seal of God upon their foreheads, and we know who they are and how many there are. No man, to be sure, can number them, and yet they are numbered, and we are told exactly how many have come out of every tribe. This is the knowledge not of man, but of God. How much greater heaven's knowledge thus suggested to us is than that suggested by the Judgment Day ! It is not now the martyr soul whose information indicates what the world has come to enjoy, not the condemned spirit before the bar of God, but the knowledge of God Himself, to whose eye no one in the great multitude of His children will be overlooked or forgotten, any more than now any sparrow falls to the ground without His notice.

It is not strange that this picture of heaven precedes as well as follows the opening of the seventh seal.

When there yet remains but one more barrier to the perfect knowledge of God in the earth, it will not be far from a heavenly state. But one more barrier to be thrown down—and what then? What is that *silence* which is represented as reigning in heaven for the space of half an hour after the opening of the seventh seal? What but the hush of perfect agreement which will at last come over this stormy world when the last obstacle to a complete acquaintance with divine truth is removed? How can men any longer dispute, when all see facts and truths in the light of a general acknowledgment? What more beautiful emblem could have been given of the final triumph of truth over error? When that glad day comes, and eye sees to eye all over this broad earth, the voice of envenomed controversy will have forever ceased, and for the first time men will be calm enough and still enough to hear distinctly the still, small voice of the oracle of God in their hearts and in creation.

VII.

THE FOUR TRUMPETS.

We have reached perhaps the most difficult part of the Apocalypse. There is no portion of the Word of God which comes any nearer to driving expositors to despair. Any gleam of light upon the darkness of the passage just before us ought to be doubly welcome. Alford frankly confesses that he has "never seen in any Apocalyptic commentator an interpretation of these details at all approaching to verisimilitude; never any which is not obliged to force the plain sense of words or the certain course of history to make them fit the requisite theory."

If I cannot speak thus strongly it is because I have seen one interpretation which Alford had not seen, that of Dr. Justin A. Smith in his recent commentary. No one can say that he either forces the plain sense of words or the course of history to make them fit his interesting interpretation of the first four trumpets. If I do not adopt it altogether, it is not because I do not perceive its reasonableness and its singular harmony with the facts of the Christian era, but because my own interpretation, already made before seeing Dr. Smith's, still seems to me preferable and even capable of including his and deriving confirmation from it.

The description of the *seven trumpets* begins with

the second verse of the eighth chapter, and continues to the end of the eleventh chapter. Each trumpet except the last is followed by something of a malign nature. First the earth is smitten; then the sea; then the fountains of waters; then the sun, moon, and stars. These disasters are followed by the announcement of three others still more dire, which are called *woes*, only two of which, however, are actually described. The first is an irruption, from the pit, of horrible supernatural locusts, which are permitted to torment men for a limited period, stated as five months. They are described with great minuteness in all the dreadful combination of their horrors. The sixth trumpet is followed by a woe still more tremendous. A vast army of supernatural horsemen, numbering two hundred millions, is seen to emerge from the region beyond the Euphrates and flow, in an awful deluge of war, over the rest of the world. Upon the sounding of the seventh trumpet we are again in heaven hearing the glad tidings that "the kingdoms of this world are become the kingdoms of our Lord and of His Christ."

Now the question at once arises, Are we to take these dreadful appearances literally or symbolically? Everybody acknowledges in a general way, and must acknowledge, that the Apocalypse is a book of symbols. But here, as in many other places, many would interpret literally—that is, they interpret literally as far as they can, and abandon a literal interpretation only because it becomes impossible through the extraordinary character of the symbols. Thus the portents of the fifth and sixth trumpets are such as to drive any literal interpreter to distraction; the locusts and the horsemen are too strange to permit them to be regarded as actual beings. But the evils of the first four trumpets, the injury done to the earth, the sea, the fountains, and the heavenly bodies, can be taken with more or less literalness, and Alford insists that they must be. He thinks that these four trumpets describe judgments inflicted upon the ungodly "by vitiating and destroying the ordinary means of subsistence, and comfort, and knowledge."

What such literal judgments could possibly be it is quite impossible to imagine. Alford has not ventured to suggest, except regarding the third, the injury done to the fountains, that it may possibly consist in the turning them into fire-water—*i.e.*, ardent spirit. The word "knowledge" in the above quotation looks as if Alford himself might have dimly conjectured that the heavenly bodies of the fourth trumpet might be metaphorical, the sources of human wisdom rather than the material sun, moon, and stars.

In accordance with this tendency to literal interpretation, the trumpets are regarded as trumpets of *judgment*. They are supposed to announce judgments by which God will chastise the wicked and advance His kingdom. In this view the key-note of the whole book is the prayer of the martyr-souls under the altar, as described in the fifth chapter, for vengeance upon their persecutors. The whole book becomes an account of the temporal judgments visited upon the ungodly in answer to that prayer. We are thus taught that the grand means by which God is to set up His kingdom upon earth is the inflicting of misery upon mankind. The last book of the Bible becomes a rehearsal not of the triumphs of the Gospel, not of the progress of truth in conquering error, not of the wonders of grace and mercy, but of the use of physical power in overwhelming men with material misfortunes. The Apocalypse thus interpreted becomes the description of a protracted Judgment Day.

It is impossible to deny that there is a measure of truth in these views. God does undoubtedly accompany His Word with such exertions of physical power as are needful, and His "terrible things in righteousness" often answer the prayers of His people for help and deliverance. It must even be admitted that in the latter part of this book, in what may be termed the era of judgments, these providential visitations upon men are exhibited as the crowning evidence by which God is to confirm and establish His Gospel. But to make the whole book a description of almost nothing else than judgments, to look at it chiefly from this point of view, is, it seems to me, a mistake which must quite prevent any clear and satisfactory conception of its most important teachings.

I object to this method because it is inconsistent with itself, continually shifting from a literal to a metaphorical interpretation as its necessities compel it. If the book be symbolic it is symbolic everywhere, and everywhere we are to look not for literal statements, but for pictures which at once veil and suggest the real meaning. I object because this method makes both the prophecy itself and God's dealings with the world unworthy in character. I cannot believe that a prayer for vengeance is the ruling thought of this book or of the Church of the latter day, still less of the glorified spirits of the martyrs. I cannot believe that a kingdom of light and truth set up, in the first place, and carried on thus far mainly by the preaching of the Gospel and by the power of love and goodness, is to be considered as winning its principal triumphs by means of physical force and temporal judgments. I cannot think that the key to the Apocalypse was hidden obscurely in the fifth chapter and in the account of the fifth seal instead of being placed where it belonged, in the very door of the building, in the introduction of the prophecy. It does not seem possible that the opening vision—that of the divine Sun, with its associate stars and candlesticks—has so little significance as to stand at the head of an account of physical judgments rather than at the beginning of the story of the world's enlightenment. For all these reasons I am compelled to reject this scheme of interpretation, and seek for a better.

What necessity is there for considering the trumpets to be trumpets of judgment? Is there no other idea for which they will stand? How will they do for symbols of the *preaching of the Gospel?* Were they not such in the days when the priests blew the silver trumpets to usher in the glad jubilee year? "Blessed are the people," we are told, "who know the joyful sound," by which I suppose to be meant an allusion to those same silver trumpets. Taking the seven trumpets of the Apocalypse as a symbolic preaching of the Gospel by the angels, we get an idea in delightful harmony with my conception of the book, and are led to expect information of something which is to be a result of the lighting up of the world with Christian knowledge.

There is appropriateness in such a representation here. The opening of the seals I have explained as the removal of great obstacles to the progress of the truth. That is the negative side of the matter. It is appropriately followed by a description of the positive proclamation of the good tidings and certain results which it is to produce.

That these results should seem to be evil, and be so exhibited, is due to the fact that the preaching of the Gospel is portrayed as it appears to *men*—*i.e.*, the unregenerate, unspiritual world, instead of the spiritual Church, which is qualified to see these results in a brighter and truer light. It will be noticed that even the final triumph over which heaven rejoices, and of which no disastrous phase is shown, is yet called a *woe*, but it is a woe only to those who are emphatically and purely "*inhabiters of the earth.*" This fact may help us to gain the point of view from which to see all the visions of the trumpets in their true light, as successes and advances to God's cause, and as woes only to its adversaries. What is "a sword" to the opponents of the Gospel is "peace" to its friends. The same truth and the same events which are a "savor of death" to one party are a "savor of life" to the other party. The path to a nation's freedom is over the prostrate forms of its oppressors, lit by the lurid light of sacked and burning palaces and blazing thrones. And in like manner the progress of the truth in the world is to be seen largely by the destruction which it works; it must appear to all who do not understand its mission only as some ruthless force, carrying havoc into peaceful scenes and overturning settled order, that "He whose right it is may reign."

Having adopted this idea of the trumpets, so much more agreeable to Christian feeling and so much more harmonious with the general tenor of Inspiration, we are rewarded at once by a further harmony of the happiest kind. For the blowing of the trumpets is preceded by a ceremony of the burning of incense. The incense is explained as that which adds acceptableness to the prayers of "*all the saints.*" This certainly cannot be a reference to the cry of the martyr-souls for vengeance in the description of the fifth seal. It is a broader cry than that, in which the suppliant voices of all saints everywhere unite. Christ's churches all over the world are not crying for vengeance; they never did, even in the darkest days of persecution. The prayer in which all without exception join must be, "Thy kingdom come!" Christians everywhere and always pray for the success of the Gospel. We are here reminded that the Gospel wins its triumphs when, and only when, it is accompanied and preceded by the prayers of God's people. The seven angels are not permitted to do their symbolic preaching until the Church has prayed and the incense has been offered. An idea so harmonious with the teaching of the Scriptures elsewhere may well encourage us that our interpretation is treading upon firm ground.

There is nothing to conflict with our idea that the sounding of the seven trumpets is a symbolic preaching of the Gospel in the fact that all the woes described come from *above*. Surely truth comes from above and Gospel light, as well as judgments. "Every good gift and every perfect boon is from above, coming down from the Father of lights." The preaching of the Gospel, in all the various ways in which it is done, may be regarded as a continual descent of heavenly blessings. Christ ascended on high in order that He might give gifts unto men. From His exalted seat He bestows with royal hand the Holy Spirit, apostles, prophets, evangelists, pastors and teachers, and all the spiritual gifts of the new dispensation. It is the down-pour of these celestial benefits which causes light and knowledge and goodness to increase in the earth.

I have already explained the fact that in this description these celestial benefits take on the forbidding aspect of "woes." To those who persistently oppose and reject them they become curses instead of blessings. Even to those who finally accept the Gospel its first aspect is ungracious; it has to wound and kill before it can make alive. But this very wounding and killing is progress toward life; after the weeping which endures for a night "joy cometh in the morning;" the very wrath of the persistent opposer, and the misfortunes which he draws down upon his own head, God makes to praise Him by the use to which He puts them in the advancement and establishment of His blessed cause in the earth. It is from the elevation obtained by such considerations that we are able to look upon the smoke of the great moral battle and hear the shrieks of the wounded and the dying and preserve our composure, and even observe with gladness that the forces of evil are pressed steadily back toward final and complete discomfiture.

So much being offered in a general way, let me now do what I can to account for the special form which is given to the results here ascribed to the preaching of the Gospel.

It is agreed by all that four of the trumpets have a general likeness, and should be considered as a class by themselves. They can be so treated by regarding them as pictures of Christian experience, or, indeed, of an experience which is much broader than the Christian, inasmuch as great numbers share the convicting and condemning work of the truth and of the Spirit who never pass on to its happier stages.

The *first* trumpet may set forth the inevitable effect of Gospel truth upon the mind in the change which it produces in the view taken of *earth as a dwelling-place.*

The ungodly mind regards this world as its home. There is so much that is beautiful and pleasant about the world that this is not difficult. While conscience yet sleeps, while animal delights are freely enjoyed, there is nothing to prevent the mind from regarding earth as its paradise. But the Gospel comes to disturb this dream, to make life real, and earnest, and solemn because responsible, and to transfer the paradise of man to a future state of existence. This result is not unskilfully depicted in the effects of the first trumpet. What happened to the land of Egypt in the plague of hail comes upon every man's land when these changes of sentiment have been wrought in the mind. It is as if hail, fire, and blood had fallen upon the earth in a desolating shower, destroying its green grass and its pleasant trees. What are more important in the furnishing of earth to be man's dwelling-place than the trees and the green grass? A man is thoroughly at home when he dwells within his own smooth lawn and under his own vine and fig-tree. If the green grass and the shade-trees and fruit-trees should be destroyed men would begin to look for some other home. And thus when the Gospel has sufficiently awakened and enlightened the mind for it to see earthly things as they are, it forever abandons the plan of making this world a sensual paradise, and takes up its staff to become a pilgrim to a better country.

If, however, the mind should still cling to its illusions and seek merely to escape from its causes of disturbance by some intellectual flight, it is met and harassed by the truth after the similitude of the *second* trumpet. Upon the sounding of this trumpet a great disaster is represented as befalling the sea. A burning mountain falls into it, turning a part of its waters into blood and destroying its shipping. We think of the sea as a great highway used by flagrant sinners as a means of escape from justice. Across the sea the prophet Jonah hoped to escape from God and from duty. Such attempts may vividly illustrate the effort of the human mind everywhere to escape from the thought of God and the consideration of its great responsibilities. But as the Gospel is preached and heard such mental flight becomes continually more difficult. It is as if the plunge of a fiery volcano into the ocean had convulsed it so as to render navigation, to the sinner, dangerous and well-nigh impossible.

The ships of the sinner are destroyed. The great ideas of the Gospel are in his mind, and though he "take the wings of the morning and dwell in the uttermost parts of the sea," or even make his "bed in Sheol," God is there. The places of escape and refuge become even more terrible than the places where truth assails him, and he has no choice but to stay at home. One cannot flee from the divine presence, for that presence is everywhere.

Shut up thus to the truth, and compelled to confront it, the soul that is still disobedient experiences a further apparent misfortune symbolized by the *third* trumpet. A star called wormwood falls from heaven and embitters the springs and fountains from which men drink. What can this be but the coming of some truth into the mind to make bitter its sources of happiness and refreshment? "Truth held in unrighteousness" becomes perverted and distorted, and yields distress and injury instead of comfort and help. It only needs that one should know enough about material and unholy sources of enjoyment to make them very bitter to the soul. They give so much more pain than pleasure that the mind turns from them in disgust and weariness. But the sorest punishment which befalls persistent unbelief is that good and true means of happiness lose all power to charm, and become only vanity and vexation of spirit. To a disordered nature everything which God originally contrived for man's enjoyment is without relish, or even nauseous and revolting.

The climax to this painful experience is reached under the *fourth* trumpet. It shows the sun, moon, and stars smitten so as to be partially darkened. The heavenly bodies have been taken everywhere in this exposition as symbols of divine illumination. There is no reason for regarding them otherwise here. The extremity of human distress is produced when the highest means of good become means of evil and causes of injury. When the commandment which was ordained to life proves to be unto death; when the Bible, and the Saviour, and the Holy Spirit become objects of terror instead of comforters; when the sun of revelation, and the moon of secular learning, and the stars of friendly Christian guidance are darkened and refuse to give their light, it is a " great and terrible day of the Lord," in which sinners are overwhelmed with consternation and sink down in despair. This is a continual result of the preaching of the Gospel, and through it as a preparation we pass into a condition of peace and joy. All confidence in every reliance except Christ must perish, and the soul have absolutely no resource but to cast itself at the foot of the Cross to perish, if it must perish, only there.

Let no one say that this interpretation of the four trumpets is unworthy because it applies them to an individual experience. One soul is worth more than the whole material world, and the phases of that mental progress by which the Gospel brings a soul to Christ are worthy to be delineated by the sublimest imagery. But it is not necessary thus to confine the application. The history of one human experience is the representative of many; we are to regard the changes of mind set forth by the four trumpets as occurring in many minds, wherever the Gospel extends. For great and constantly-increasing numbers of men is it true that the green earth of a natural life ceases, under the dreadful storm of Gospel truth, to be the paradise that it was; the sea of thought and imagination is no longer a thoroughfare of escape from conscience after the terrible mountain of burning truth has fallen into it; the sources of sensual pleasure and even of rational delight become embittered when the wormwood of divine accusation is mingled with them, and even the very orbs of religious light shine with a baleful glare when they shine upon the head of an unpardoned, unrepenting sinner. These experiences, so sad and so wretched, are the very steps by which great multitudes of men find the joy of a believer.

Would it be strange if what takes place in the mental life of an individual, and occurs broadly in the experiences of many of the same generation, should be found to occur also through great epochs of history, so that the historical student shall be able to discover something like the succession of the four trumpets in successive periods of the Christian era? It is not at all strange. The education and progress of the world, which it takes many centuries to accomplish, resembles the education and progress of a single soul, which is effected in a lifetime. What the mental philosopher sees transpire in the stages of an individual mind, the historian sees take place as the human race passes from a more youthful and inexperienced period to one more mature and well informed.

This is where I would place Dr. Justin A. Smith's

interpretation of the four trumpets. He looked for their historical application, and found it, it seems to me, with remarkable clearness. The period of the first trumpet he considers to be that dreadful time in the first century when their mad opposition to Christ made the Jews the virtual destroyers of their own beloved city and their own favored land. Out of that pleasant land they went by thousands to drudge as slaves in every country. The Jew has been a homeless wanderer ever since.

The second trumpet Dr. Smith makes to be the overthrow of the Roman Empire. That was, indeed, an event worthy to be represented by the image of a burning mountain falling into the sea. It was chaos come again, a mighty disaster in one way and as mighty a benefit to the world in another. No doubt Christianity had much to do with that overthrow; it was necessary that the kingdom of iron should give way that the kingdom of heaven might take its place. "The stone smote the image upon its feet, and brake them to pieces."

The third trumpet Dr. Smith considers to be the heretical teaching by which the truth was so perverted in the first Christian centuries. Nothing could fit the symbolism better. A star falling from heaven and becoming wormwood, and embittering streams and fountains, is a fit image of truth losing its correctness and poisoning the life of those who had received it. The mischief thereby done is immeasurable, but the benefit to the cause of Christ is also immeasurable. It was necessary that truth and error should thus grapple and be in deadly conflict, for the superiority of the truth to become manifest. Pilate's question, "What is truth?" could never be fully answered in any other way. We know now what is truth because we know what is not truth. Having tasted the bitter fountains, we know which are the sweet.

Finally, Dr. Smith's fourth trumpet is the *Dark Ages*. One has only to hear the name to feel the fitness of the figure. The heavenly bodies are not represented as wholly but only as partially eclipsed, and yet even a partial eclipse makes the earth a dreary place. The obscuration of truth during the Dark Ages was dreadful. The great dignitaries of the Romish Church were ignorant and often infidel. The priests and monks made a jest of their callings. The people knew only what filtered to them through these gross mediums. But the way to something better lay through all this darkness, and having suffered this nightmare once, it may be hoped the world will never have to suffer it again.

VIII.

THE FIFTH AND SIXTH TRUMPETS.

The results of the preaching of the Gospel symbolized by the four trumpets are of a similar character, and are evidently intended to be regarded as a whole. The results of the following trumpets are of quite a different kind, and are described with so much elaborateness of detail that the entire ninth chapter of the Apocalypse is occupied with the fifth and sixth trumpets. An account of the seventh trumpet is deferred until the close of the eleventh chapter.

There is a similarity between the descriptions of the fifth and sixth trumpets which makes it proper that they should be treated together. My idea of their significance is that they relate to two classes of opponents of the Gospel which its spread unwittingly but inevitably produces.

The first class is represented by swarms of supernatural locusts, which come up out of the bottomless pit to do their bad work in the world. These swarms are let out of the abyss by a fallen star—that is, by a fallen angel, to whom is given the key of that abode of evil, and who uses it to let that evil loose upon mankind. First rises from the pit a dense volume of smoke, which darkens the sun and the air, and then appear prodigious locusts—locusts like war-horses, with crowns of gold, human faces, woman's hair, lion's teeth, iron breastplates, wings, and tails like scorpions. Their power to hurt is said to be in their tails; the time of their prevalence is five months; and they have a king over them whose name is Apollyon, which is the Old Testament term for perdition.

With regard to these locusts, Alford says, "There is an endless Babel of allegorical and historical interpretations of these locusts from the pit. The most that we can say of their import is that they belong to a series of judgments on the ungodly, which will immediately precede the second advent of the Lord; that the various and mysterious particulars of the vision will, no doubt, clear themselves up to the Church of God when the time of its fulfilment arrives; but that no such clearing has yet taken place a very few hours' research among histories of Apocalyptic interpretation will serve to convince any reader who is not himself the servant of a preconceived system."

Notwithstanding this unfavorable augury of the success of any attempt to open this passage I shall make the venture, believing that the materials for such a venture have already been provided by others. It is certainly possible to point out many remarkable coincidences between these descriptions and facts which have already occurred, the perception of which must cause us to doubt the correctness of Alford's opinion that it still remains for the future to disclose the meaning of these prophecies.

There has always been a strong disposition to recognize the historical prototypes of these strange locusts in the Saracens, the followers of Mohammed. Like the locusts of Egypt, these Saracens swarmed over upon the world from Arabia. Like the locusts of Egypt, they settled upon large portions of the Christianized earth and reduced it to its original desolation. It seems to me that while we may not say that these alone, exclusive of other like enemies of the Gospel, are meant, we may say that the locusts of this passage are intended to represent a class of which the Saracens are the most prominent example.

Mohammedanism is now generally regarded as a Christian heresy rather than as an original and independent religion. It is as truly such as Romanism, differing from it not in kind, but only in the degree in which it mingles Christian truth with pagan error. It is well known that Mohammed had a dim and confused idea both of Judaism and of Christianity, and that he borrowed and corrupted what he knew of both systems. What could more fitly represent this fact than a star falling from heaven, an angel shooting from his celestial sphere and becoming the opener of the bottomless pit? The half truth contained in their new religion was just the impetus needed to arouse the latent forces in the hearts of the Arabians, and precipitate them in a fiery deluge upon the Christian world. It is inevitable that the Gospel should be misunderstood and incorrectly reported by human ignorance and perverseness, and that such misunderstanding and perversion should become the most tremendous opposition to the Christianity from which indirectly it has its derivation. Thus has it been with Moslemism, and for centuries it settled upon and ravaged the fairest parts of Christendom, and still continues its ravages.

Parts, at least, of the description of these monstrous locusts are strikingly suggestive of Moslem peculiarities. The locusts are like war-horses, and the Moslems have always been notable for the grace and power of their cavalry. The Arab is most at home and most terrible as a warrior when in the saddle. The golden crowns, the human faces, the woman's hair, the lion's teeth, the breastplates, the wings, are all not inappropriate descriptions of that strange people, whose fierceness and success in war is not more remarkable than their feminine love of luxury and splendor, and their rapid progress in art and civilization. That the locusts have Apollyon for their king may well set forth the fact that the Moslems have been organized and led by great kings and generals, whose genius for war and government could scarcely have been greater if they had really been diabolical.

One other item of the description calls for special notice. The hurtful power of the locusts is located in their scorpion-like *tails*. In the vision which follows the very opposite statement is made—that the situation of hurtful power is in the *heads* of the creatures described—a contrast which must have special significance. Its force seems to be that the Saracenic enmity to Christianity is not to be regarded as eminently intellectual. The fact is, that Moslemism was spread not by conviction, but by force; not by the power of ideas so much as by the power of the sword.

So many points of agreement between these strange symbols and the form of error to which I have referred can hardly be accidental coincidences. Without pressing them it is safe to say that in this passage

Inspiration probably had in view all that class of anti-Christian opposition of which Moslemism is a chief example. The truth, from both Jewish and Christian sources, which has been vaguely reported in heathen ears and mixed with an overpowering quantity of heathen superstitions has darkened the world like swarms of locusts from the abyss, and blighted wide regions where once the Gospel had been known in its purity. It can hardly be thought probable that a prophetic book intended to foreshadow the future of Christianity from the first century to the end of the world could have left out of sight either Moslemism or the class of delusions to which it belongs. In that class Romanism must be placed, for it clearly comes under the description given. If it be thought strange that the peculiarities of that description are not such as to indicate Romanism rather than Moslemism, I may reply that elsewhere the papacy receives extended notice, while if we consider either the widespread havoc wrought by the religion of Mohammed, the prodigies of its history, or the vast extent of its present empire, we cannot think it could possibly have been quite omitted from the prophecies of the Apocalypse.

But the next vision is even more appalling. It is ushered in by expressions of unusual apprehension. Upon the sounding of the sixth trumpet a voice is heard from the horns of the golden altar commanding to loose the four angels bound in the great river Euphrates. The loosing of these angels is said to be accurately determined as to the year and the month, and even the day and the hour. They are no sooner

THE FIFTH AND SIXTH TRUMPETS.   95

loosed than they turn to a mighty army two hundred millions strong—an army of horsemen who wear breastplates which appear red, and blue, and yellow. The horses have the heads of lions, out of whose mouths pour fire, and smoke, and brimstone. These volcanic mouths are fearfully destructive, but these horrible horses have the power to hurt with their tails also. Their tails are like serpents with heads, so that a lion's head kills at one end of each horse's body, and a serpent's head hurts at the other end. The extent of the destruction produced by this strange army amounts to so much as a third part of men.

What we are to understand by this description Alford ventures no suggestion of, except in the most general way. He, however, defends the propriety of taking the geographical designation ("at the great river Euphrates") literally, even though all beside must be considered mystical. He compares with it the allegorical passage, "Thou hast brought a vine out of Egypt," in which, although "vine" is to be understood allegorically of the Hebrew nation, "Egypt" is a location to be literally taken. We are under obligation to Alford for settling for us at least so much about this vision, that its territorial situation is in the region of the river Euphrates.

Beyond that historic river lies that vast hive of nations toward which the civilized world has but lately begun to look with the gravest apprehensions. The foremost squadrons of the mighty army capable of being recruited there, to the number of two hundred millions, have already arrived in the United States, and inspired such fear that a barrier has been raised by law to keep their main host out of the country. The danger distinctly seen by even the less thoughtful is that the swarming myriads of Eastern Asia will pour over the lands and nations of the West, and reduce the better conditions of the more enlightened of mankind to their own low level. These fears are largely for material good and selfish advantage, but the nobler part of the Western world has fears of a nobler kind. The Church fears that China and India will deluge Christendom with pagan ideas, and thus overthrow every vestige of Christian institutions.

Such fears would be in the highest degree reasonable had not the Bible furnished us with counter-assurances, and especially here with a sufficient warning of the evil and a prediction of its limitations. We are not permitted to think that it has gathered its awful force and is to break loose upon its destructive mission without divine knowledge and divine appointment, and being under divine control. We are particularly assured that it comes upon the world at the very instant intended, and at the bidding of the voice which speaks from the horns of the golden altar. Is not that golden altar the altar of prayer, and must not the voice which issues from it be the voice of God in answer to the prayers of His people? We must not lose sight of the fact that this dreaded human irruption is, first of all, the loosing of the angels who are to fly to bear the divine message to the four quarters of the earth. Christ can never have His own while such a large part of the human race remain shut up and shut away from the influences which revolutionize character elsewhere.

There is, then, something divine and angelic about this pagan flood of which we are so afraid. It is the inevitable result of the principles and preaching of the Gospel, that the walls which have so long separated the Eastern nations from the rest of the race should be broken down, so that the peoples of the earth shall flow together as one mighty sea. The result at last will be the grand brotherhood of mankind, but for a time it will prove disastrous to many human souls. Though it is the loosing of the angels who stand for the welfare of the whole human race, as their number (four) betokens, for a time it may appear only like the march of a resistless army of enemies to ravage and destroy the whole earth.

It may, perhaps, seem a doubtful identification to see in the colors (red, blue, and yellow) of the breastplates of the horsemen the recognition of that love of gaudy hues which characterizes barbaric nations, and of which we are reminded by our tea stores as well as by the robes of Oriental ambassadors. If it was worthy of the Holy Spirit to speak of the colors at all, it is not unworthy of an interpreter to try to find some meaning in them. One remembers also that red, blue, and yellow are the three prismatic colors which, united, compose that pure white light in which objects are seen clearly, but which, separated from one another, deceive the eye and confuse the understanding. In this way the fact may be symbolized that the power of Oriental nations to resist the truth is in those distorted and false ideas which they already have. Certain it is that we do not err in making much of the fact that the power of these horsemen to hurt is in their *heads*. We have already seen the probable significance of the fact that the locusts do their mischief by means of the stings situated in their tails. Mohammedanism is not credited with very much mental power. But not so with the Oriental peoples. They are represented as *three*-headed, like the Cerberus of the ancients. Each horseman must be supposed to have a head of his own, a human head, while each horse has a lion's head and also a serpent's head at the end of his tail. Such an exuberance of heads is very striking. It must be that in this way it is intended to suggest the remarkable intellectuality of the Eastern nations.

They are, indeed, keen and subtle in intellect, and they have philosophies, and theologies, and cosmogonies of the most elaborate and pretentious sort. So formidable are they as antagonists in debate, that missionaries among them need to be trained and highly accomplished disputants in order to contend successfully with them. It is well known that poets, and novelists, and scholars of the Western nations are fast importing the ideas of the East, claiming that in these are to be found a higher wisdom and a better gospel. This is the real fight between Orientalism and Occidentalism; this is the great invasion of the East into the Christianized West. While it is to be feared, and even expected, that many minds will be paganized and many souls destroyed, the end is not doubtful. It is as certain that Christianity will conquer as it is that it has already conquered on every kind of battle-field, and that it has the power of God's own truth.

IX.

THE VISION OF THE TRUTH.

The traveller through dark and difficult paths, in which his way is much of the time doubtful, is reassured if at intervals he catches sight of the sun, or of the stars, or of earthly way-marks by which the correctness of his course is made certain. Thus may we rejoice and take fresh courage at this stage in our perplexed journey of interpretation, at beholding the vision in the tenth chapter of the Apocalypse. The clouds break away and we see once more the familiar face of that sun whose cheering beams gave the light which shone upon our original starting-point.

For such substantially is the vision of another mighty angel now described as coming down from heaven with a cloud for his mantle, a rainbow about his head, his face like the sun, his feet like pillars of fire, a little book open in his hand, and standing majestically with his right foot upon the sea and his left foot upon the earth. Surely it is not difficult to understand the meaning of this magnificent figure. Not exactly identical with either of the previous representations of the great spiritual sun of the universe, it yet so combines the previous with new features as to suggest to our minds just the facts which are needed for our comfort and encouragement at this point in the prophecy.

Let us see where we are. Six out of seven of the trumpets which symbolize the preaching of the Gospel have now been sounded. We cannot be far from the grand consummation. But we have had two terrific descriptions of mighty armies of foes whom the very progress of the Gospel itself must inevitably raise against it. Against these swarms of human locusts, against these hundreds of millions of Oriental horsemen, what power can stand? How can it be possible that light and truth are to conquer so much error and darkness? The answer is this new vision of the truth in such beauty and grandeur as to light up the gloom of the prophecy and dispel its alarming suggestions. Thus, we are taught, in the day prefigured by the prophecy, the truth is to overcome its myriad enemies and accomplish its remaining task in the world.

I consider, then, the mighty angel of the tenth chapter as a beautiful symbolic representation of the sublime situation which the knowledge of the Lord will have attained, even while menaced by the myrmidons of ignorance and error in the last days.

Notice with what care and skill the symbols of previous chapters are here united to show the identity of this with those. This mighty angel is clothed with a *cloud*, which revives the recollection of the Son of man in the prophecy of Daniel as well as of the Son of man in the first chapter of this book. In both cases the coming seen was in the clouds of heaven, and the meaning of the appearance was that the kingdom was to be a heavenly one from above rather than below. To this revelation was added by the vision of the Son of man in the first chapter, that the kingdom was to be one of light. That was what the sun, the stars, and the candlesticks signified. The face of this angel renews that teaching, for it is like the sun. Then there is a rainbow round about his head like that around the throne in the vision of heaven. In that vision there was a book—the symbol of the communication of truth—in the hand of the Father, and here the mighty angel has a little book open in his hand. It is a *little* book, and it is *open* to show that now, after so many seals have been broken and so many trumpets have been sounded, the task of the truth in the world is comparatively small and comparatively easy. We have thus combined just the symbols which are appropriate to represent the situation of great power which the truth will have attained at that advanced stage of the world's progress which the prophecy has now reached.

This mighty angel stands with one foot on the sea and the other on the earth. What is this but a position of universal sovereignty? When he speaks it is as with the voice of a God, for seven thunders are heard, and the thunder is God's voice. When God spoke to His Son the people said that it thundered. The angel lifts up his hand to heaven and swears by the eternal Creator that delay shall be no longer, and that one more gospel trumpet shall finish the mystery of God according to the good tidings which He declared to His servants, the prophets. What can be implied by all this but the entire removal of that veil which has been spread over the minds of all people? We have now reached a point in the development of the kingdom of heaven when the end is in sight. Truth has so nearly completed its conquests that victory is assured. Its reign has become so nearly universal, its principles are so widely accepted and understood, that the moment of its complete ascendancy seems near at hand, and the task of removing earth's remaining error comparatively small. It is as if the godlike figure of this chapter were actually visible to mankind and the vast majority of human beings prostrate in adoration and submission.

The means by which the final clearing up of human perplexity is to be effected is the remaining fact of this chapter. As in the former scene it is the Lamb who takes the sealed book from the hand of the Father and is hailed as the agent of its publication to mankind, so here it is the prophet who receives the little book from the angel. The agency of the Church in the enlightenment of the race in the last days is thus emphasized. More and more must the children of God share with their Master His blessed conquests. The kingdom and the greatness of the kingdom is to be given to the saints of the Most High. Out of Zion, the perfection of beauty, God is to shine. They who have themselves been first taught of God are to be the teachers of the nations.

An interesting distinction is here made between the communicable and the incommunicable knowledge of a Christian. Every Christian knows far more than he can impart or than it is proper to communicate to others. That which was uttered by the seven thunders the prophet seems to have understood, and would have published it had he not been restrained. He was told not to write it, but to seal it up; like that which Paul saw in the third heavens, it was not lawful to be uttered. On the other hand, he was invited to take the book and to make it his own by (mentally) devouring it, and then he was given to understand that he was to "prophesy again over many peoples, and nations, and tongues, and kings." Thus widely was he to make known what he had received from the little book and what had become to him a matter of both sweet and bitter experience. Thus is the world to be thoroughly evangelized in the last days. Its preachers will speak out of a profound knowledge of God. As the mountains rest upon foundations buried deep in the earth, so their proclamations of truth will leave unspoken more than they express. Was it not thus with Jesus? Did He not often imply that He had left unsaid more than He had uttered?

But the message that is uttered in the last days will be eminently a message which comes from a thorough experience of its truth. It will be no hearsay Gospel, like that of the seven sons of Sceva, "We adjure you by Jesus, whom Paul preacheth." There is too much of that sort of preaching, and it is worth very little. The world can never be converted to God by such preaching. The preachers of the latter day cannot possibly be of that sort. They must be such men as are here described, who have so eaten and digested the great doctrines of revelation that those doctrines have passed into their spiritual circulation and affected every part of their natures. They must be men who know thoroughly both the sweetness and the bitterness of the facts of life, and who can speak to their fellow-men out of a sympathetic realization of what the truth must be to all who receive it. When the world enjoys such preaching, the preaching of profound knowledge and of personal experience, the end will not be far off.

X.

THE CHURCH AND THE WORLD.

Is it not just what we might expect at this point of the prophetic narrative to have our attention called to the condition and magnitude of the Church? Up to this point nothing has been directly said about it. Six of the trumpets which represent the preaching of the Gospel to the world have been sounded; we have been shown the effects of that preaching upon the human mind, and in stirring up against itself different classes of opposers; the end is evidently near, and surely it is time that the relative situations of the Church and of the world should be shown.

Accordingly the Apocalyptist now receives a measuring-rod, and is told to "rise, and measure the temple of God, and the altar, and them that worship therein. But the court which is without the temple leave out, and measure it not; for it is given unto the Gentiles: and the holy city shall they tread under foot forty and two months."

In this picture we have the well-known features of ancient Jerusalem used to portray the condition of the Church in the world far on toward the great consummation. Let us not be discouraged; let us rather be encouraged when we find it substantially the situation at the present time. The different degrees of ceremonial sanctity which attached to the Jewish temple, with its altar and priests, the court which surrounded it, and finally to the city of Jerusalem, are here used to picture the condition of the Church in the latter part of the era represented by the sixth trumpet. The temple itself was too holy for any but the priests to enter; Gentiles might enter the court, and yet it was regarded as a sacred place, while the whole city, though open to all kinds of strangers and given up to all the common uses of life, was yet the *holy* city, because in it the temple of Jehovah stood, and compared with other cities it was a sacred city.

In like manner we are now bidden to regard the world. The process of its enlightenment has now gone so far that it may all be regarded as a holy city. True, good is not everywhere appreciated; there are yet many human swine who tread the pearls of truth under their feet. But there is a temple—that is to say, a church—in the world, whose worship is pure and whose dimensions are great. For this must be what is meant by the direction to measure the temple, and the altar, and them that worship therein. It is a challenge to notice the magnitude of the proportions which the Church has now reached, and its vast and growing influence; while, on the other hand, the prohibition to measure the court or the holy city is a disparagement of its importance, an intimation that the non-Christian element is something too insignificant to be measured. The pure Church of God, the temple of living stones which Christ will by this time have reared in the earth, is to be regarded as the great fact of the earthly situation. Next to this fact is that of a court round about the temple—that is, a congregation in close proximity to the Church, which, although not yet to be counted as positively Christian, is yet permeated with Christian ideas, and so near to the kingdom of heaven that but a few steps, and for some but one step, is sufficient to cross the interval between congregation and church. Then, last of all, there is the holy city itself—that is to say, a world all parts of which have become so acquainted with Gospel truth, so leavened with Christian knowledge, so familiar with the presence and example of the Christian Church, that every zone and every land may be said to be in sight of it. What though the court be given to the Gentiles—that is, what though congregation be yet dominated by worldliness and the holy city be trodden under foot, which means the presence and power of evil in the partly evangelized world? The time of the wicked is comparatively short; it is limited to a period here called forty-two months; and when this period shall have ended, the congregation will all have joined the Church, and the holy city of the world will have become as sacred and pure as the temple itself. Then "Holiness to the Lord," once the inscription upon the mitre of the priest, will be engraved even upon the bells of the horses, and all common things will have so passed within the sanctified sphere of true religion that the difference between temple and city will cease to be perceived, and the contrast between Church and world will have ended.

And now, for the bringing about of this glad time, the importance of one branch of Gospel preaching is emphasized. It is the force of the *testimony* which the truth is to receive from the witnesses who come forward to prove it Let us not fail to observe that the final triumph of the Church and the Gospel is here attributed to the cumulative force of the *evidences of Christianity.*

Any light which can be thrown upon the description of the two witnesses contained in the eleventh chapter ought to be very welcome, for Alford tells us that " no solution has ever been given of this portion of the prophecy." He means, of course, no satisfactory solution. It is, indeed, a most perplexing passage, of whose meaning most interpreters have been able to give hardly any intelligible idea. Two witnesses clothed in sackcloth are to prophesy for a period of twelve hundred and sixty days. They are described in the language of the prophecy of Zechariah as two olive-trees and two candlesticks standing before the Lord of all the earth. They have power to destroy their enemies by fire from their mouths, to shut up the heavens as Elijah did, and to smite the earth with plagues like those which Moses brought upon Egypt. Upon the completion of their testimony the wild beast from the abyss is to kill them, and their corpses are to lie unburied upon the street of the great city, called spiritually Sodom and Egypt, for three and one half days, insulted and exulted over by their enemies, until the spirit of life from God enters into them, and they experience a wonderful resurrection and ascension into heaven. The final result is a great convulsion of nature, the destruction of seven thousand, and the enlightenment of the remainder so that they perceive the glory of God.

It is not strange that the historical interpreters have been at their wit's end to find in past events something suitable to such a description. We have seen that Alford brands all attempted solutions as worthless. He especially remarks, regarding the ascension of the witnesses, that no attempt has been made to explain this by those who take the passage figuratively. He inclines to a literal interpretation, insisting that the two witnesses must be two individuals probably yet to appear upon the earth ; but he seems not at all troubled by the difficulty of making the prodigies ascribed to them literal. Of course the fire from their mouths, the miracles and plagues, the death, resurrection, and ascension must all be actual facts upon Alford's supposition. It is impossible, it would seem, to make a wilder conjecture than this.

Upon the theory that the theme of the Apocalypse is the progress of the truth in the enlightenment of mankind, and that while the breaking of the seals represents the removal of obstacles to that enlightenment, the blowing of the trumpets represents the preaching of the Gospel, it is both consistent and forcible to find right here a symbolic description of the history of the evidences of Christianity. Christianity can never become universal until it is proved to be the true religion. The progress of that proof has not been constant, but fluctuating, and sometimes it has met with reverses almost equal to a death, from which it has experienced a subsequent resurrection. That the argument is to go on until all mankind are fully convinced, that facts and evidences are to accumulate until doubt becomes impossible, and the truth of Christ's religion has ascended, as it were, to a heaven where it is no longer assailable—this is just what we all hope and believe, and this is just the kind of history and the only history which could be fitly represented by the symbolic narrative before us.

Thus interpreted, this passage treats of exactly that phase of the great subject of the book which we might expect in this particular place. It puts just the emphasis which it deserves upon the cumulative power of the evidences of Christianity in the last stages of the great contest. When the whole world stands at length in the same relation to the Church which the holy city had to the temple, when the knowledge of the Gospel has reached the remotest bounds of the habitable earth, what is to quicken the progress of the great cause to the actual possession of the heathen as its inheritance? What but the establishment of the claims of our divine religion beyond all doubt or controversy? When it can no longer be doubted that the Bible is a revelation from God, when Christ can no longer be denied the honors of divinity, and when the other great facts and doctrines have ceased to be debatable, we may surely expect that the Holy Spirit will use this certainty for the rapid and complete conversion of the human race. The progress which we now see in the gathering of confirmation from all lands and all sciences is the swelling of a flood which must ultimately sweep from the earth all scepticism regarding the divine origin and authority of Christianity.

The number *two*, which has seemed so puzzling in this passage, may be explained as the least number which is sufficient to make testimony convincing. "In the mouth of two or three witnesses every word shall be established." Christ insisted that His testimony was valid because the Father corroborated it: there were two witnesses. Elsewhere the candlesticks which are employed to light up the darkness of earth are seven in number; here they are two, to agree with the law of testimony.

And really the proofs by which Christianity is being established in human confidence are derived from two sources—Christian learning and secular learning, or the Bible and nature. God has revealed Himself both in His Word and in His works, and the students of both revelations supplement and corroborate each other's conclusions. When Christian scholarship shall have borne witness to all that it has learned about the truth, the scholarship of the world will be found supporting it with the results of all the sciences and the fruit of all the philosophies.

This twofoldness of the evidence is here emphasized in language adapted from the prophecy of Zechariah. "These are the two olive-trees and the two candlesticks which stand before the Lord of the earth." Here are *four* witnesses instead of two to be identified, if we make the witnesses individuals. But the simple principle already stated explains the difficulty on the ground that each of the two great divisions of Christian evidence has a twofoldness in itself. Christian learning taken by itself has a complexity of proof which is self-supporting, and secular learning is of many kinds which mutually sustain each other. If, now, we say that the two candlesticks represent Christian learning and the two olive-trees secular learning, how appropriate and beautiful are the symbols! How true to fact is the description of the prophet in which the oil from the olive-trees was seen to flow through tubes directly into the candlesticks! Zechariah had but one candlestick, for then there was only the Jewish Church; John had two, for in his time the Christian Church had been added. But into both the Jewish and Christian candlesticks the oil of the older revelation through nature has continually flowed. "The heavens" as well as the preacher "declare the glory of God;" "day unto day uttereth speech, and night unto night showeth knowledge;" and all that nature says in any of her provinces and all that scholars learn in any of their researches, are constantly being added to the evidence that Christ is the Lord and Saviour of the world.

The explanation of the prodigies wrought by these witnesses is as easy, according to this idea of their character, as it is difficult according to any other. Two literal, fire-breathing, individual men would be monsters such as never yet were seen and never, probably, will be seen upon the earth except in the simulation of Chinese jugglery. This fire going out of the mouth is no more to be taken literally than the sword going out of the mouth of the symbolic Son of Man. In both cases the mouth is to be taken as the organ of speech, and the fire is the convincing power of the argument issuing from the mouth. Of course the death produced is logical rather than physical, and the statement that "if any one is minded to hurt them, he must *in this manner* be killed" seems like a careful guarding of the reader against taking the death spoken of too literally.

The description proceeds to attribute power to the two witnesses to shut up heaven as Elijah did, and to bring plagues upon the earth like those which came upon Egypt. This means, of course, that the evidences of Christianity are to have the same overwhelming power to silence contradiction as in the cases of Moses and Elijah. We are reminded of the success with which Elijah, single-handed, confronted and overcame the four hundred and fifty priests of Baal, with almost the whole nation in sympathy with their idolatry. And how, long before, Moses and Aaron went into the presence of Pharaoh and his magicians and humbled all their pretensions. Such is to be the triumph of Christian evidence in the days that are to come. No subtlety of intellect, no array of human learning, no combination of error and sophistry shall be able to stand before it.

This triumph, however, is not to be obtained without many a hard-fought battle and many apparent reverses. To disprove the truth, the wild and savage spirit of unbelief is represented under the figure of a wild beast emerging from the abyss. This wild beast makes war with the witnesses and succeeds in killing them. We know this wild beast well; it is the ancient figure of worldly empire, ruling by brute force, and inspired and sustained by Satanic malice and cunning. It is inevitable that this malign power which has tyrannized over and terrorized mankind for so many ages should do its utmost to prevent the complete enlightenment of the world. All worldly and hellish dominion survives only as long as the night of human ignorance, which is the cover of its real character, endures. We have already seen many a struggle between this bulwark of error and the dawning and growing truth. We shall, perhaps, see many more and some so violent and powerful as for a time to make it seem as if the truth had been finally overthrown. There have been hours and periods of darkness in which such doubt was thrown upon the Bible, and Christianity was so generally discredited as to appear about to be driven from the world. Voltaire thought that he should be able to crush the religion of Christ. Such periods of depression are so melancholy that they may well be symbolized in the passage before us by the death of the two witnesses.

Yes, and by the forlorn spectacle of their poor, helpless corpses lying unburied on the street of the great city exposed to the taunts and gibes of their many enemies. If ever Christianity shall seem for a time to be destroyed from the earth, we may be sure the malice of its enemies will never suffer it to be decently interred and so put out of sight and out of mind. No, the exultation of unbelief is like the savage joy of the Indian warrior, who cannot be satisfied with the bloody recollections of his victories, but must needs wear the scalps of his conquered foes dangling in a hideous necklace under his very eyes. The open street of the great city is the public knowledge of the world. If Christianity should seem to be proved a delusion all the world must know of it. The part of the world which will gloat over it will be the wickedest and most unbelieving part of mankind.

The "great city" here brought to view is the same world which, at the beginning of this chapter, was characterized as the "holy city." There the world was considered in its best aspect as the place in which the temple of God is being built, and as affected by the Church, salutarily, to its remotest bounds. Here the same world is considered in its worst aspect, in its attitude of opposition to the Church, and of resistance to all saving influences. That this is the correct identification of the great city we may be sure from the remaining items of description. It is the "great city which spiritually is called Sodom and Egypt, where also their Lord was crucified." No literal city can satisfy all the terms of this description. It must be a city enough greater than Jerusalem to combine the characteristics of Sodom and Egypt, and also be recognizable as in the largest sense the scene of our Lord's crucifixion. Sodom is in history the place of unbridled lust, while Egypt is the land of pagan and earthly wisdom. Was not our Saviour slain by the combination of these two—the rage of sensuality in the gratification of fleshly appetites, at the same time exulting in the superiority of its intellectual attainments? The people who have these characteristics make up that great city on whose open street the corpses of the two witnesses are left unburied. Another indication of character is afforded by the statement that those who gloated over the unburied witnesses did so "because they (the witnesses) tormented them that dwelt on the earth." Wherever in the wide world men are tormented by the growing proof of the truth of the religion of Jesus, there are the streets of the great city, of which the literal Jerusalem, in its apostasy from God, is only one of the smaller wards.

The resurrection and ascension of the two witnesses is a beautiful representation of the final confutation of all unbelief and the permanent establishment of the truth of Christianity upon an impregnable foundation. The time is to come when the proofs of our religion will go up like their Lord, in a cloudy chariot, to the heaven of ascertained and unquestionable fact. When that day comes the destruction which will befall the advocates of all forms of error will be sudden and irremediable. It will be like the ruin which overtakes men in the earthquake shock and the falling city. "Seven thousand" will be slain outright— that is, *all* the thousands (for seven is the number of perfection) who have opposed by doubt or disputation the advancing demonstration of the truth, will be logically destroyed. Not a tongue will continue to wag in denial of our divine religion. When these are silenced the rest, the vast number of spectators of the contest, will become affrighted and give glory to God. They will have that fear of God which is the beginning of wisdom, and over all the earth there will be none foolish enough to say, as infidels have said, that the heavens declare the glory only of astronomers like Copernicus, and Kepler, and Newton. Wherever the day dawns upon a child of the human race, or night draws the curtains which hide the stars from the gaze of man, there the united power of the two witnesses, Nature and Revelation, shall be acknowledged irresistible, and the eye shall look upward only to adore.

We have now reached the end of the sixth trumpet, so much the most remarkable of all in the range of its developments and the greatness of its successes. The story of the *seventh* trumpet, like that of the seventh seal, is comparatively brief and uneventful. Not that it is really less important and glorious, but for the same reason that the history of peace is so much shorter than that of war. "Happy the people who have no annals," it has been said. We have now reached the time when, all obstacles having been removed, the Gospel has only one unvarying record of success which can be told in a few words. In the account of the seventh seal we had that single touch of the heavenly silence for half an hour—a silence which stands for the blessed hush of controversial tongues and the ceasing of all mockers from their unholy ribaldry. The seventh trumpet is a pæan of victory; great voices herald through heaven the grand tidings that the kingdom over the world (Alford's translation) is become our Lord's and of His Christ.

There is little more which calls for explanation. Again we see the four-and-twenty elders upon their thrones, and they fall upon their faces and give God the glory of the triumph. Last of all the temple of God is opened to disclose the ark of the covenant, and to remind us that all the wonderful developments of the divine kingdom, down to the latest ages of time, are only the fulfilment of God's plighted word to the fathers, and were really as sure to take place when the promise was first given as when they were actually occurring.

XI.

THE CHURCH AND THE DRAGON.

It is the happiness of a true theory to find continual corroborations in the facts for which it attempts to account, and at each step of its progress to meet recurring the appearances which gave it plausibility at the outset. It is pleasant to be able to call the reader's attention to the reappearance, at this point in our study, of the symbols which gave us such assurance at the beginning. The introduction, it was said, with its flaming figure of the King, as a sun, attended by stars and candlesticks, promised a vision of the lighting up of the world by means of truth. What could the symbols mean but illumination? What could the prophecy be but that of the spiritual enlightenment of mankind? We have now followed this clew through half the book, and it has seemed to serve us; we have not felt lost in the labyrinth. In fact, at the end of the eleventh chapter we appear to have reached the termination of the dramatic action, and to have completed our task successfully.

Instead of ending, however, the prophecy now enters upon a new series of visions, the relation of which to the preceding appears to be that of an episode of the sixth trumpet. It would not have been strange, nor would it have cast any doubt upon our interpretation thus far, if, at this point, we had come to an entirely new class of symbols, showing a radical change of subject. But there is no change, for, as if to reassure us that we are still to go on with the same clew, at the outset of this new departure we meet again with the same symbols which we have learned to understand so well. This new series of visions, then, as well as the preceding series, must have for its subject-matter the spiritual enlightenment of mankind, since, as at first, the figure chosen to hint their purport is a magnificent composite *light-bearer.*

No one can fail to see, when once his attention is called to the fact, that, at the beginning of what may be called the *second part* of the Apocalypse, we have, substantially repeated, the splendid figure of the first chapter. That was "one like unto the Son of Man," with His countenance "as the sun," "in His right hand seven stars," and surrounded by "seven golden candlesticks." Now we have "a woman clothed with the sun, and the moon under her feet, and upon her head a crown of twelve stars." These symbols are all light-bearers, and must mean here just what light bearers meant there, *the story of the truth,* in its battle with falsehood for the possession of the world. The differences in the two pictures are such as to indicate the modification of treatment of the subject at this point. The first part of the Apocalypse makes the *King* of the kingdom the light of the world; the second part treats of the *Church,* the bride and queen of the King, as the luminary. The story now to be told is how the Church is to hold forth the word of life, and shine as a light in the world, and what are to be its difficulties, trials, reverses, and final and glorious successes.

The drama of the twelfth chapter, now to be explained, is as follows: The woman, clothed with the sun, and crowned with twelve stars, is described as being in the pains of childbirth, when a terrible enemy to her and to her offspring appears, in the shape of a great red dragon. This dragon has seven heads and ten horns, and seven crowns upon its seven heads. So mighty is the monster that, with one sweep of its great tail, it casts down a third part of the stars of heaven. It stands before the woman to devour her child at the instant of its birth; but the child, a man-child, which is destined to rule all nations with a rod of iron, is caught up to God and to His throne. War is now represented as raging in heaven itself, between Michael and his angels and the dragon and his angels, which results in the casting of the dragon, with his angels, out of heaven. He is now called the old serpent, and still more plainly, the Devil. There is loud exultation in heaven because the accuser of the brethren before God is cast out, and because of their victory through the blood of the Lamb, and by the faithfulness of their testimony, and by their heroic martyrdoms. Woe is declared to the inhabitants of the earth and the sea, on account of the embittered wrath of the Devil, and his knowledge that his time is short. The dragon now persecutes the woman, but to her are given two wings of a great eagle, with which she escapes to the wilderness, to be nourished there a time, times, and half a time. The serpent next casts out of his mouth a flood of water, to carry away the woman, but the earth helps her by opening its mouth to swallow up the flood. The dragon at last abandons the contest, but continues to show his implacable spirit by warring with the rest of the woman's seed.

This remarkable description, which equals a Greek or Hindoo myth by its apparently wild and fantastic images, has been the puzzle and the despair of most commentators. They have been quite unable to find in it any connected and consistent sense, and have felt obliged to torture both Scripture and history for any plausible solution, or to take refuge in the unrevealed possibilities of an inscrutable future. They say that the time may come when this chapter will have an intelligible meaning, but that time is not yet. If, after such confessions, the theory of this exposition yields a rational and harmonious sense for the entire chapter, it ought to go far to establish the idea of the purport of the Apocalypse here followed as the correct one.

Not but that many interpreters have caught glimpses of light here and there, but they have failed to get a complete view, as it seems to me, because they had no standpoint sufficiently high to comprehend all the parts of the action. Great trouble has sprung from the attempt to blend a literal interpretation of some of the details with a figurative interpretation of others. There are points in which the narrative so closely agrees with historical events as not only to seem to have been suggested by them, but even to demand identification with them. Such points of agreement are the birth of the man-child and the birth of Christ; the catching up of the child to God's throne and the ascension of our Lord; the war in heaven, which results in the casting out of Satan and the history of the Devil and his angels; the escape of the woman to the wilderness and the exodus of the Israelites out of Egypt into the wilderness of Sinai. These resemblances have tempted, and, indeed, seemed to compel interpreters to identify the symbolism with the history which it so closely imitates. They even insist that there can be no other explanation. Alford is so sure that the man-child of this chapter is the child Jesus that he warmly denounces all interpretations which do not assume their identity. The latest commentaries that I have seen follow him in accepting this identity as indisputable.

The difficulties, however, are so great, to my own mind, of harmonizing such an identification with the other details of the vision that I wonder how its advocates can be so positive. If the man-child be Jesus of Nazareth, then the woman must be the Virgin Mary, and the Roman Catholics have scriptural authority for enthroning the Virgin with all the signs of divine dignity. They have not been slow to claim the passage and to make the most of it. If, on the other hand, with Protestants generally, we regard the woman as the *Church*, then Jesus of Nazareth becomes the child of the Church instead of its father, as He is represented in Heb. 2 : 13, "Behold I and the children which God hath given Me." To avoid this difficulty the Church has been extended to mean the Church of all ages; but whatever we make of it, it can be only in a *figurative sense* that the Church can be called the mother of Christ; and if the mother be figurative, may not the child be most probably figurative also? That it is so is evident from the next great difficulty, which is the wide discrepancy between the histories of this man-child and of our Lord. For the man-child is caught up to God and made secure from his enemies from his very birth, while Jesus remained upon the earth till manhood, and ascended only after His foes had inflicted upon Him all the suffering He was capable of enduring at their hands.

These disagreements are so great as to forbid the attempted identification, and yet it may be freely granted that the resemblances to the history of our Lord are such as to make us feel that some reference to Him is intended. The simple and satisfactory explanation of this puzzle I believe to be this. Jesus is *the Truth*, as well as the Way and the Life, and the fortunes of the truth in the world are so much like Christ's personal history, that when they are detailed, they remind us of it. It is not at all strange that His truth should fare as He fared, that it should be in peril from some Herod, have to hide itself in the wilderness as He did, and have the power to ascend into heaven and sit down upon His throne. "I am the Truth," He said, and as the Truth, He is continually living over again the life recorded in the Gospels, being born of a woman, assailed by enemies, hiding in the deserts, being crucified, rising from the tomb, and ascending into heaven.

We thus gain the point of view necessary for the satisfactory interpretation of the vision—satisfactory because intelligible, harmonious, and approximately complete. If it be not quite possible to explain all the particulars, it is possible, at any rate, to give a rational account of most of them.

Most interpreters have seen that the woman must represent the Church, but they have failed to see the peculiar character in which the Church is here exhibited. It is that of the Teacher and Enlightener of mankind. All the details of the vision may be harmonized with that special aspect of the Church, though it is impossible to harmonize them with any other. The history of the Church's struggle to instruct the world is set forth in this symbolic narrative so vividly, that it is easy to trace its stages; and if the historical interpreters had had their eyes upon this phase of the past, they would not have been so bemired.

The appropriateness of the symbols by which the Church is suggested to us in this character, as the teacher and light of the world, is obvious. "Clothed with the sun!" What a pity to belittle this sublime metaphor, as some have done, into a figurative description of a lady's bridal dress! It is rather the assertion that the Church's wisdom is the wisdom of Christ Himself; that she has power to teach the race because in her resides the knowledge and through her shine the splendors of the Great Teacher, the sun of the first chapter of the Apocalypse. The moon and the stars have their appropriateness in being also light-bearers, and it may be said that in this symbolic representation the Church is invested with *all* the celestial luminaries. There is no light which heaven can give which is not at the disposal of the Church. It has Christ, the great sun of Revelation; it has the stars, twelve in number. This number, the product, it is said, of three and four—three being the number of heaven and four being the number of earth—implies that angels and saints, the great created intelligences, the star-intellects of both worlds, are at the service of the Church. As for the moon under the feet of the woman, what can that be but *secular learning*, which is always waxing or waning, and which, though sometimes quite dark, at other times sheds a clear and silvery radiance, of unspeakable comfort and use to mankind? Sun, moon, and stars all belong to the Church, and all aid her to accomplish her great mission, as the teacher of the human race.

The birth pangs—what are these? Is there a teacher who does not recognize the fitness of the figure? When scholars are dull, when minds are perverse, when understandings are prone to mistake error for truth, how hard the prophet labors to put his message in such form as to meet the exigency! Early in the history of the Church the fact was recognized that the doctrine about Christ needed to be put into statements so clear, so precise, so guarded, and yet so full, that it should be impossible, henceforth, to confuse the belief of the Church with any one of the many forms of heresy which equally claimed to be of scriptural authority. The need was imperative, but it was not found easy to supply it. It took three centuries of study, meditation, and controversy to accomplish the task. At the Council of Nicæa, the creed was finally and conclusively formulated. A statement of the nature of Christ and of His relations to the two other persons of the Trinity was then published to the world, which has been ever since, and is destined, evidently, to remain through all time the authoritative interpretation of the scriptural teachings about our Saviour.

Such a fact is abundantly worthy, it seems to me, to be described as the birth of a man-child from the labor-pains of the Church. It was, in the realm of thought, a duplication of the birth of Jesus in the realm of life. The final publication of the right doctrine concerning His unique personality was a kind of second birth into the world. The creed was, indeed, a man-child; was caught up into a heaven of impregnable safety from the moment of its birth; was seated upon a throne, and is destined to rule all nations with a rod of iron, inasmuch as it is, undoubtedly, a correct statement of the facts of the divine trinity, which mankind must accept, and with which they must harmonize themselves.

Should any demur to the putting of such honor upon the creed of Nicæa, there is an alternative interpretation which admits of no such objection. It may be said that the first great task of the teaching Church was the production of the New Testament, and that this part of the Holy Scriptures was the man-child. All that has been said of the Nicæan Creed is of course true, and true, in a still higher sense, of the New Testament. The opposition to that book, the heaven of acknowledged inspiration to which it ascended, and the authority with which it has ever since ruled over the minds of men, all fit the symbolic description, and may be accepted, if it seems preferable, as a satisfactory interpretation of the account. It is really inclusive of the other.

Turning now to the symbols of hostility to the

Church as a teacher, and to her mental offspring, the appropriateness and, indeed, necessity of such symbols are at once apparent. Who would be most averse to a clear, exact, doctrinal statement of the person of Christ, or to the publication of those inspired documents from which that statement has been drawn, but that old serpent, the Devil, who is the father of lies, and whose kingdom depends upon the continuance of intellectual as well as moral darkness over the earth? He is described as a great red dragon, a monster with seven heads and ten horns and seven crowns, whose mighty tail sweeps a third part of the stars of heaven from their places. A great deal of thought and study has been wasted upon the question how ten horns could be placed upon seven heads. The question implies that it is necessary for us to clearly picture these symbols before the eye of the mind in such a way that nothing shall be out of proportion or offend the taste. The assumption is unwarranted. Can anybody make a picture of the Son of Man with a sword coming out of His mouth which would not be grotesque and repulsive? Our task is not that of the artist, to get natural and pleasing pictures out of these descriptions, but rather that of the reader of hieroglyphics, who disregards the impossibility of the combinations as facts, and regards them merely as symbols of spiritual truths, incapable of representation in any manner less extravagant.

Without stopping, then, for any such child's play as the placing of three superfluous horns, we have merely to inquire how the combination of symbols in the dragon represents His history, resources, and spirit. It occurred to De Wette that the heads might be emblems of sagacity and the horns of power, while Delitzsch tells us of "a great serpent with seven heads" which is found in the Assyrian inscriptions. We need go no further to see that the Devil is here represented, in accordance with ancient usage, as the god of this world, uniting in himself all Satanic cunning with all mere human sagacity, and having at his command all the means of earthly power. It is this formidable being, whose first stupendous success was to deceive and draw from their steadfastness a third part of God's own angels, and who is red with the blood of uncounted human souls, who opposes, with eager and unsleeping malice, the further enlightenment of mankind by the Church. The seals would not be broken if he could prevent it; the trumpets of the Gospel would not be blown if he could hinder; the clearing up of the obscurity which attaches to the great facts of existence is precisely that act of the Church which will be most fatal to that empire which is founded upon ignorance, prejudice, and misunderstanding. No wonder Satan is stirred to utmost wrath when the mind of the Church is being inspired to produce those Gospels and Epistles which constitute the clearer part of Holy Writ. No wonder he is wrathful when the mind of the Church is big with the conception of the exact relation of the Son of God to the Father and the Holy Spirit.

What, now, is the war in heaven? Of course not literal war, nor literally in heaven; not the actual clash of arms between Michael and his angels, and Satan and his wicked cohorts. But something on earth worthy to be represented by such a Titanic contest.

What can that be, if not the contest in the visible Church concerning true and false doctrine? What an awful fact it has been, and still is, that among the professed followers of Christ there has been a wide difference of opinion on fundamental points, and that that difference has produced estrangement, sectarianism, and bloody persecutions! What could be more fitly described as "war in heaven" than this? Who could deserve to be branded as the minions of Satan if not the mitred and crosiered inquisitors of the apostate church? And who have fought with a courage and an intelligence worthy of the angels themselves if not the martyrs who have contended so earnestly for the faith once for all delivered to the saints? When John Huss went to the stake, dressed in garments covered with pictures of the fiends of whom he was accused of being possessed, and, calmly disregarding the slanders of his enemies, committed himself and the truth which he had taught to the keeping of a faithful Creator, he showed a knightly prowess which the Archangel Michael himself might be glad to be able to exhibit. A few such facts are all that is needful to justify the claim that the history of doctrine has been like a war in heaven.

We have not yet reached the end of that war. There is yet enough of it to make us glad to know that it is certain of a happy termination. We realize something of the blessedness of him "that readeth and (those) that hear the words of this prophecy," when we accept its forecast regarding the issue of this conflict. This passage assures us that Satan is to be cast out of heaven with all his followers. That means that the dark spirit of error is to be banished entirely from the Church, so that its members shall all be of the same mind, and there shall be no more sects and no more schisms. When that time comes it will be worthy of a celebration. Not only in heaven, but upon earth, certainly everywhere among God's people, will be heard the exultant declaration—"Now is come salvation, and strength, and the kingdom of our God, and the power of His Christ: for the accuser of our brethren is cast down, which accused them before our God day and night." When "the cruel war is over" within the Church itself, and the best and wisest teachers of the faith are no longer maligned as errorists and fanatics, and the bad spirit of deceit is left entirely to the unchurched, the kingdom of God will, indeed, have come, as we have never seen it yet and can scarcely imagine it to exist upon the earth.

Meanwhile, during the era of contention, misunderstanding, and persecution, with false doctrine and a paganized Christianity in possession of the civil power, what would become of the truth and its loyal confessors but for the power which they possess of hiding themselves in obscure places, where they can bide their time to issue forth? Something like this must be meant by the two wings of a great eagle which were given to the woman, that she might make her escape to the wilderness. It is well known that when the Bible became a forbidden book and a New Testament church a forbidden institution, both Bible and Church found a refuge in obscure hamlets, in remote and inaccessible wilds, where they lived on unknown by the world, while centuries passed and a better day drew on.

The water which the serpent cast out of his mouth after the woman, to carry her away, must be that flood of calumny which has been poured upon the godly by those who have made the public opinion and written the histories of mankind through all the dark ages. What simple-hearted and faithful company of true believers has there been which has not been so vilified as to appear like a crew of dark conspirators against human happiness? This systematic and persistent aspersion of the excellent of the earth is one of Satan's chief devices for prolonging his empire. But, blessed be God! the earth helps the woman by opening its mouth and swallowing up the river of misrepresentation. In time the lie is found out, and witnesses arise, both in the Church and out of it, who testify to the character of real well-doers. History vindicates the martyrs, science comes to their support, scholarship, both secular and sacred, establishes the correctness of their doctrines and the purity of their principles, and so at last it comes to pass that truth, though it has been "crushed to earth," rises again, while "error, wounded, writhes in pain and dies among her worshippers."

The final action of the defeated but implacable dragon has greatly puzzled those who have sought to explain it. After his discomfiture by the woman and her offspring he departs to make war with the "remnant of her seed, which keep the commandments of God, and have the testimony of Jesus." Who the remnant of her seed are, it is difficult to say upon any other theory of the purpose of the Apocalypse than the present one. But how easy upon this! If the man-child be some great doctrinal statement, like that of the Nicæan Creed, concerning the divinity of Christ, the other offspring of the woman are other formulated truths. With any or all of them the Serpent is at war, and when he is not attacking one he is assailing another. Nothing could be truer to fact than the representation that having been worsted in his conflict with the teaching of the Church regarding the first great doctrine to be formulated, he has contested every other doctrine in its turn. As he opposed the divinity of Christ in the third century, so he opposed justification by faith in Martin Luther's time and the new birth in Whitefield's. He maintains the fight with truth somewhere, anywhere, where he can find a mind not yet established in the faith. We may be sure that the father of lies will never relax his energy or retire from the field while there is yet a corner of the world where the whole truth is not yet known. Nothing less can ever end his campaigns than the knowledge of the Lord covering the earth as the waters cover the sea.

XII.

THE WILD BEASTS.

The portrayal of the opposition which the Church must encounter in its endeavors to enlighten the world passes, in the thirteenth chapter, from Satan himself to his most formidable emissaries. In this chapter two wild beasts are described and their relations to each other and to the father of lies distinctly set forth, with the extent of their tremendous and apparently successful resistance to the truth.

It is a pleasure to have reached a point where the agreement of the best expounders is so marked that, in a general way, we may accept their conclusions. The description of these beasts is so easily comprehended that it is impossible not to recognize their originals. The one which rises up out of the sea, in some respect resembling a leopard, a bear, and a lion, but with seven heads, ten horns, and ten crowns upon his horns, and on his heads names of blasphemy, is the well-understood symbol of *worldly power*. The different animals, blended into one, are the several universal empires of the ancient world, which passed the sceptre on from one to another, until, at the time at which the Apocalypse was written, Rome held it in its iron hand. The fact, suggested by this symbol, is, that the greatest adversary, next to the Devil himself, which the truth has to meet in the world is the terrible opposition of political power.

It is this special idea that interpreters seem to me to have failed to grasp. No one can help seeing that, in some way, the political systems of mankind are represented as antagonizing the Church. One who lacked the general conception of the Apocalypse which I have set forth would be likely to think that the war between the Church and the worldly power here in view is along the whole line. And so, indeed, it is, but with special emphasis upon the conflict of truth with error, the Church trying to educate the race, and organized political power setting itself against such an education. The prophecy was that when Christ's people should go out into the world to instruct mankind in heavenly knowledge, they should find, right across every path, forbidding further advance, the combined strength of civil government and human worship of political power.

That it is worldly power in this aspect of its character—namely, its opposition to human enlightenment, that is intended, is evident from the description. Of that description, the most significant part, the part which agrees most with the other descriptions of the Revelation, is that the wild beast had upon his heads "names of blasphemy." What are names of blasphemy but falsehoods about God and slanders against Him? The wild beast of worldly power is depicted, then, as wearing upon its awful front, and bearing it high over the world, the denial of God's blessed truth. In addition to this, later on it is said that "there was given to him a mouth speaking great things and blasphemies." "And he opened his mouth for blasphemies against God, to blaspheme His name, and His tabernacle, even them that dwell in the heaven." What could be more explicit than this? What could be more appalling in the divine characterization of worldly power? Of all the dreadful things which can be said of worldly empires, there is nothing so dreadful as the fact that they antagonize the Revelation from heaven and the teachings of Christianity.

Well was it for the early Church that it was so plainly forewarned what it would have to meet. Well was it that it could not be surprised by the apparent success of worldly power in neutralizing the Gospel. It was told that the wild beast would make war with the saints, and overcome them, gain universal dominion over the minds of men, and command the worship of all whose names are not written in the Lamb's book of life.

How natural, and even necessary, such a result seems! How imposing is great worldly power! What an awe-inspiring fact was that of a throne which ruled the whole civilized world! How adapted to bring the selfish heart into a grovelling submission and a base adulation! Tiberius, or Caligula, or Nero could speak the words of life or death; they could reward sycophancy with the revenues of provinces or bid the most illustrious citizen open his own veins and die. Everybody knew that the whole great system rested upon fraud, that Tiberius was the greatest liar in the world, as well as the greatest sovereign. What of it? What but the deification of falsehood? If lying answer so good a purpose, lying seems divine.

This, perhaps, was the spirit in which Pilate asked his famous question, "What is truth?" What, indeed, must truth have seemed to Pilate as an instrument of selfish aggrandizement? He had no use for it. To know how to dissimulate cunningly, like Tiberius, his imperial master—that would be more to the purpose. And so, like most veteran politicians from that time to this, he deliberately chose falsehood rather than truth, and worshipped the Devil rather than God as the founder of the State. Has not diplomacy come to mean the art of skilful lying? How much "good Queen Bess" thought it necessary to use that kind of diplomacy! Napoleon reached the climax with his military falsehoods, until the world learned to say "False as a bulletin!"

Such facts make lucid the statements of this chapter regarding the wild beast of empire. That "the dragon gave him his power, and his throne, and great authority" is an unveiling of the base measures to which civil rulers have owed their ascendency. The tremendous reverses and revolutions in which many a worldly hero and many a great government have seemed about to perish, and then by some brilliant feat or some fortunate turn have been lifted to greater glory than before, have been among the greatest occasions of human wonder. When the Roman Empire appeared to dissolve, and then presented itself again in the form of the Papacy, it is not strange that the world should have "wondered after the beast." It is not strange that men, who are so prone to worship success, however obtained, should worship both the beast and the Devil who could give such power to the beast. This was the foe which the Church had to meet when it set out to make men wiser and better, a foe armed with all the weapons of the State and enthroned in the servile admiration of mankind for all successful villainy. What could show "the patience and the faith of the saints" more signally than to maintain such a conflict, often at the expense of "captivity," and often at the cost of "death," with no loss of confidence in those spiritual weapons which were ultimately to prove "mighty through God to the pulling down of strongholds?"

But the trials of the champions of the truth were not to prove greatest under the dominance of the pagan Roman Empire. It is with reverential admiration that we see that, centuries before it actually occurred, inspiration clearly foresaw that change in the ruling power, which, when it did take place, was so disguised as to deceive the very elect. Oh, that Christians had understood the warning which, to our eyes, appears so clear! For that the second wild beast, coming up out of the earth, having two horns like a lamb, but speaking as a dragon, is the description of papal Rome few can doubt.

It is not necessary, however, to confine the prophecy to the Papacy. The substitution of two lamb-like horns for the seven heads and ten horns of the first beast speaks of a change of policy in worldly powers, of which the change from pagan Rome to papal Rome is a prominent example. It is the change from a rule of sheer, brute violence to a rule bolstered by fraud and cunning. Pagan Rome proudly said that might made right, and it would rule because it was the strongest. Papal Rome covered the iron hand with a silken glove, and while meekly pretending to be the servant of Jesus of Nazareth, riveted its fetters upon the minds and hearts of men, content to obtain by fraud what it lacked the force to seize.

All candid persons must recognize the faithfulness of this prophetic portraiture of the Romish Church. No uninspired mind could have anticipated the prodigy, which even now seems too great to be real. That the Papacy came to "exercise all the power of the first beast" through the fiction that the Pope is God's vicegerent is a matter of history. That this imposture was and is supported by the pretended ability to work miracles everybody knows. Everybody may not so distinctly see that the great crime of Romanism has been to cause those who dwell in the earth " to *worship the first beast*, whose deadly wound was healed." What else could be the effect of that mighty ecclesiasticism which lifted the Pope, often a man from the humblest ranks, up into the position of a god, and set his cardinals and bishops among and above princes ? There has never been any system among men which tended to strengthen their love of pomp, their servility before power, and their faith in imposture like Roman Catholicism.

The adaptation of priestcraft to serve the ends of selfish ambition is, of course, an old story—as old as Egypt and her priestly kings. Every great oppressor, from Nimrod to Napoleon, has thought to strengthen his tyranny by taking advantage of the religious instincts of the people. Priestcraft has buttressed despotism by adding to the temporal perils of resistance the awful curse of God and the pains of perdition. Coming in the meek guise of a church, it has spoken like a dragon. It has kept the masses in ignorance, in order the more easily to hold them slaves. For the image of the emperor it has substituted the image of the Virgin, and perpetuated all the idolatry of paganism. It has put its brand of ownership on its unfortunate subjects in their brutal and degraded appearance. It has forbidden any who did not grovel at its feet to engage in trade, or even to live in peace at their homes. Its reign has been one of blood and fire, and its enmity to light and truth has been that of the infernal pit, out of which it came. The mission of the Church to spread the knowledge of God has met in the apostate church its most determined and implacable foe.

One of the most cunning devices of this apostate church to perpetuate ignorance and error is probably indicated by the closing verse of this chapter. It gives the number of the name of the second beast as six hundred and sixty-six. The latest and ablest students of this enigma agree that the ancient interpretation of Irenæus must be true, who found this number to be the total, according to the Greek method of enumeration, of the value of the component letters of the word *Lateinos*. So interpreted, it certainly does give its name to the most prominent example of the lamb-like beast and indicate one of its principal devices for keeping the human mind in ignorance. That device is to adhere, in all lands and in all ages, to a Latin service, and so hide even the meagre light of the Romish ritual under the bushel of an unknown tongue.

Surely Satan must be credited with so artful and deadly a contrivance to shut away the light from human minds. How effectual it has been let the records of Catholicism tell, which has had a clear field and entire ascendency now for centuries in the most illiterate countries of Christendom, such as Ireland, Spain, and Mexico. In those countries the people remain in a condition of ignorance, superior only to that of savages. The astute wisdom of the Papacy, inspired by the diabolical prince of this world, succeeded in turning the Gospel lamp into a dark lantern, available chiefly for nefarious deeds and the murder of souls.

XIII.

THE FORCES OF ILLUMINATION.

These pictures of the two wild beasts and of their resistance, so determined, to the truth are most appalling. The question is on our lips—What is the Church, and what resources has it at its disposal, that it should be able to confront such mighty enemies? How can the terrible contest be expected to end happily? With worldly power, and priestcraft, and all Satanic influences and forces leagued together to keep the world in darkness and sin, how can it ever be illuminated?

The fourteenth chapter answers these questions, by giving an interior view of the Church, its most essential qualifications to champion truth, and the great providential aids by which its success is to be accomplished.

The Church which can make headway against the powers of darkness which have been exhibited is not the strong church of modern parlance, but something quite different. Nothing is said about its wealth, social position, or the splendor of its house of worship. A kind of potency quite different is indicated by the description of "a Lamb standing on Mount Sion, with one hundred and forty-four thousand bearing His name and the name of His Father written in their foreheads." That means, of course, a *Christ-like* church, in which Christ truly dwells, and on whose countenances the saintly character is written. Whenever a soul is rescued from the bondage of ignorance and sin, its outward appearance becomes so transformed as to show the presence within it of the kingdom of heaven. The added grace and nobility which are conspicuous in Christians is one means of power over hostile forces. The names written upon the forehead of true disciples will eventually prevail against the ugly mask of the beast.

The actual presence of the Lamb with His Church is its chief strength. The nearest which the apostate church comes to this is the distant resemblance to a lamb given by its two horns. But this is only hypocrisy, while the true Church is really glorified by the Lord's presence with it and in it. This fact alone makes the Church equal to all demands, and in showing us the Lamb with His followers, inspiration quells our fears, as those of the young man with Elisha were quelled when he saw "the mountain full of chariots and horses of fire round about Elisha."

There are one hundred and forty-four thousand with the Lamb—an exact number—to represent the solid phalanx of known and enlisted light-bearers, from whom is to be expected the lighting up of the world. The items of description which follow are beautiful and impressive in the extreme.

1. *They hear and learn the heavenly harmonies.*
2. They are absolutely pure from spiritual adultery —*i.e.*, idolatry.
3. They obey Christ with the unquestioning precision of military discipline.
4. They are separate from the world.

5. They *tell no lie:* like Nathanael, they are Israelites indeed, in whom is no guile, who love the truth, the whole truth, and nothing but the truth.

The first and last of these characteristics seem to call for special consideration, though all are worthy to receive, and might profitably receive extended notice. But these are such needed traits in those who are set to be the teachers of our dull race, that it is necessary to dwell upon them.

As to the first, the Church is represented as dwelling on Mount Sion—a figure for spiritual elevation—and the top of this holy mountain is near enough to heaven to permit its inhabitants to hear and learn the heavenly harmonies. When the harpers above strike their golden harps and the celestial choir sing a new anthem before the throne, the Church on the mountain-top hear the melody and learn to sing it. There could be no happier image of the superior wisdom of Christ's true Church and its clear perception and enjoyment of revelations which the ordinary human ear hath never heard. If the Church could hear only the discordant jangle of earth's discords; if it had no means of telling which among the many sophists and disputers of this world were in the right, it would have no fitness to guide human perplexity out of its labyrinth. But an ear so fine as to catch the higher harmonies of heaven, a spiritual culture great enough to know how to bring order out of the apparent confusion and melody out of the divine operations in Nature, Providence, and Grace, is well fitted to keep itself in tune with heaven and to help all mankind to get in tune at last.

What a difference there is between persons in regard to the musical ear! One class seem to be unable to discover any distinction in sounds; another class notice dissonance where few can perceive it. To the first class all music is only noise: they cannot tell one tune from another; they cannot, by any possibility, learn to sing any tune for themselves. To the second class much that is called music is only noise; they discern the least differences in tunes, the least discord in an apparent harmony, and they catch a new tune without effort. Of course it is this latter class which must furnish the world with its music-masters. It is only such persons who can develop the musical sense in others, and train them to sing together, until all voices are in entire accord.

Now truth is the perfect harmony of facts and statements which blend and unite in the divinest agreement. To a mind trained to perceive it, the exact concord of concurring truths is entrancing in its sweetness. The cultivated Christian sense of what is delightful because it is true is forever revelling in the harmony of knowledges which come from all quarters. From history, from science, from experience, from the Bible, come announcements of the same facts, whose agreement and mutual corroboration it is most agreeable to perceive. The person who hears and enjoys these heavenly melodies is the person to teach others how to distinguish and enjoy them also. But the greater number of mankind have all this to learn. They have no nice sense of the difference between truth and falsehood, and the perpetual discord of lie fighting with lie, and misrepresentation quarrelling with misrepresentation, the horrible din of conflicting and irreconcilable assertions, does not appear to disturb them. The very sense of what is fitting in statement is yet to be awakened in their souls. When they, too, demand music instead of noise; concurrence and agreement and mutual support between fact and theory and doctrine, and the setting of earth's tunes to the music of the spheres, they can then join their voices to the grand chorus which hymns the divine praises above and below.

The last characteristic of the Church which is mentioned is its uncompromising faithfulness in teaching the truth. "In their mouth was found no lie." It will be seen that this is exactly what is needed to complete the picture of a divinely qualified corps of teachers. It is one thing to be able to perceive the truth; another to be able to tell it. There are those whose perceptions are better than their utterances; who, seeing clearly themselves, have not the courage or the grace to make known their convictions to others. But the people who are to light up this dark world are the brave generation of truth-tellers. They do not hold the Jesuitical theory that what it may be well to know for one's self, it may be politic to keep from others. They do not make the ancient distinction of the philosophers between the knowledge which should be *esoteric* (concealed) and that which may be *exoteric* (made known); on the contrary, they believe in letting the light shine and in preaching a whole Bible; they are not afraid of truth coming from any quarter, and do not understand the art of telling pious lies to those who are supposed not to be able to bear the whole truth. "In their mouth is found no lie," no half truth, no plausible sophistry, no subtle deception. They are teachers who can say of themselves what Paul said of himself, "not handling the Word of God deceitfully; but, by manifestation of the truth, commending ourselves to every man's conscience in the sight of God." Such teachers are the hope of the world.

And now follows the symbolic setting forth of certain great providential developments, by which such teaching is to have its full effect.

The first of these is the upspringing of the *missionary spirit* in the Church, and the progress of its operations until it has reached all mankind with its message. Given a church which knows the truth and is willing to proclaim it, the next thing is to send that church upon its mission to every creature. This is set forth by the vision of "an angel flying in mid-heaven, having eternal good tidings to proclaim unto them that dwell on the earth."

The second development which is to be of great service to the Church is the *downfall* of the vast *system of imposture* by which wickedness has so long maintained itself in the world. For "a second angel followed, saying, Fallen, fallen, is Babylon the great, which hath made all the nations to drink of the wine of her wrath of her fornication." There has been much discussion of the meaning of the term Babylon. It is generally supposed to refer to pagan and papal Rome. I am disposed to take it in a wider sense, of the whole immense confederacy of evil, in which fraud and violence have sustained irreligion, in its apparent successes and triumphs. These successes have astonished and confounded the human mind, and made it seem as if it were vain to serve God. Many a blundering observer of the ways of God, since and before the Psalmist, has been very much puzzled by the prosperity of the wicked, and has said, "Verily, I have cleansed my heart in vain, and washed my hands in innocency." Such appearances are great hindrances to the acceptance of the truth. But the time is coming when this hindrance will be removed. Fraud will not always be able to succeed. The time is coming when not only Rome will come to grief, but the whole bad system of building power upon imposture, all round the earth. That, it seems to me, and nothing less than that, is the fall of Babylon the great. For Rome to go down, only to be succeeded by some other form of spiritual tyranny, would be an event too trivial to be heralded by Revelation. The event celebrated here must be some gigantic, because universal and final collapse. The overthrow of all that is rotten and base in man's dealings with man may seem a great deal to promise, but it is no more than would be expected from the figure before us. "Babylon the great" must be the great world-Babylon. The downfall of any tyrant, the failure of any adventurer, the collapse of any imposture, the subversion of any system or state which has been built up and maintained by vile means, is a foregleam of what is finally to take place on the widest scale, when the whole vast fabric of successful iniquity comes tumbling down, and the thieves and liars are all exposed and recognized. How much easier it will be then to propagate the truth than it is now! Every soul will see its own best course in that day, by the light of the blazing bonfire with which the world will celebrate the destruction of the wild beasts which have ravaged the earth so cruelly.

A third development now follows which we might anticipate, the previous one being understood. A third angel proclaims the infliction of the wrath of God upon the worshippers of the beast, and of his image, and those who receive his mark on their foreheads or hands. Of such it is said that they shall be tormented " in the presence of the holy angels, and in the presence of the Lamb," with much more of the same purport.

To understand this we must ask ourselves: When the time comes that the missionary church has covered the globe with its stations, and the confederated evil of the race has reached its inevitable catastrophe, how will a man feel who continues in the old, bad ways of imposture? It is not a question of hell-fire or the torments of the other world, except as these are used to throw light upon the misery of being a persistent sinner here after the downfall of Babylon the great. We are not to waste our study on such foolish questions as whether the saved can be happy in full view of the damned? Curiously enough, in asking that question we turn from the real question of the passage, which is, How can the *ungodly* be happy in full view of a predominant godliness? The symbolism here is used to set forth the future of this present world and a state of things highly favorable to the progress of the Gospel. Such, then, will be the flourishing condition of true religion and the prevalence of genuine piety that men who go wrong will be shamed and tormented by a contrast with goodness, such as would be the case if they were vile in the presence of the angels. It will be a time whose conditions will be the exact reverse of the present, since now a wicked man can easily lose sight of all goodness whatever.

It is worth our while to endeavor, at this point, to discover the force of the statement made in the twelfth verse, which seems like a tally-mark of our progress. It is almost identical with a passage at the close of the description of the first wild beast (13 : 10), "Here is the patience and the faith of the saints." Now it is said : "Here is the patience of the saints, they that keep the commandments of God, and the faith of Jesus." Evidently in both cases a word must be supplied to complete the thought, but not the same word. In the first case, at the close of the account of the appalling success of the wild beast of worldly power in warring against the truth, and in punishing fidelity to it with captivity and death, the word to be supplied is *need;* "Here is the *need* of the patience and the faith of the saints." In the second case, at the close of this glowing representation of the time when a bad man on earth will be as uncomfortable and unhappy as if he were sinning in the presence of the holy angels, the word to be supplied is *reward;* "Here is the *reward* of the patience of the saints, they that keep the commandments of God, and the faith of Jesus." Surely, when that time comes, merely to live in it, or to contemplate it and feel that one has helped it on, will be a magnificent reward.

The natural and easy progress of this line of interpretation carries us forward to the significance of the next statement. "Blessed are the dead who die in the Lord from henceforth: yea, saith the Spirit, that they may rest from their labors; for their works follow with them." We are to take these words not so much as the description of heavenly felicity (though they are that), as of the peaceful and happy condition of the earthly Church in the good time coming. It will be like the state of the sainted dead, in its comparative freedom from toil and trial. By that time the hard work will have been done; patience and faith will have reached their reward in conspicuous and commanding virtue, and the Church will have the easy task of a successful enterprise and a victorious cause. Those who have died to self and become alive in the Lord will not need to die out of the body in order to find rest from their labors, for their works will follow with them in great and blessed results as fast as they are performed.

But one further development is needed to complete the series—a twofold development, which has been already more than suggested. That is, that the Christian teachers of the world should have troop to their aid, the accumulated consequences of all teaching, good and bad; of all actions, good or bad, in all ages. The earlier ages of the world are ages of seed-sowing; truth is disseminated of which no immediate effect is seen; principles are implanted which fail, for a time, to bring forth any proper fruit. Likewise, evil is done, error is taught, without any apparent mischief, and mankind conclude that truth and error, good and evil, have no radically opposite results. But by and by these results will have accumulated, and ripened, and manifested themselves in such a way that they can no longer fail to be seen. All that mankind have ever said or done will reach its inevitable fruition. The blessed work done by the faithful of all lands, and of all generations, will have gathered its resistless momentum, and the real character of all shams and sins will be finally and completely exposed by the calamities which they will have produced. It will be the harvest-time of the world, and men will walk in the light of the vast sum of human experience. The foolish experiments of mankind having all ended disastrously, and the wisdom of God having been vindicated by centuries of happiness and glory, the teachers of the truth will have everything to corroborate, and nothing to throw doubt on their instructions.

Such must be the meaning of the visions of harvest and vintage with which the chapter closes. As we see the "white cloud," and one sitting upon it "like unto the Son of man, having on His head a golden crown, and in His hand a sharp sickle," we behold the image of the kingdom of heaven upon earth coming into its promised inheritance of all the good for which former ages were the preparation. And as we see the angel with his sharp sickle, appointed to gather the accursed vintage of earth, and to cast it into the wine-press of the wrath of God, we may rejoice again that the evil side of human experience is among the "all things" which "work together for good to them that love God."

XIV.

THE ERA OF JUDGMENTS.

It is evident that we have now been brought by the dramatic action of the Apocalypse to the Era of Judgments. By this I mean, not the Judgment Day, but a period of earthly and temporal judgments, by which God will assist and complete the triumph of the truth in the days to come. At the beginning of the world's history judgments had an important part in the moral education of the race. The flood, the fiery storm that fell upon Sodom and its sister cities, the ten plagues which were visited upon Egypt, were all inflictions of judicial punishment by which the cause of truth and righteousness was greatly advanced. In like manner, we are here taught, God will interpose in the future. There will come a time when great and signal judgments of God upon the wicked will again come to the aid of the Church, to break down the unbelief of the world and to paralyze its resistance.

The description of the terrible vintage of human wickedness, with which the fourteenth chapter of the Revelation closes, has already introduced us to this era of judgments. But the fifteenth chapter describes its formal inauguration, and shows the fitness of all things, in heaven and on earth, for its arrival.

Again, as at each other great epoch of the prophecy, we are in heaven. The description is not full, as in the fourth chapter, but sufficient of the symbols which occur there are given to indicate the same scene. The sea of glass before the throne, and one of the four living creatures, are particularly mentioned. It was unnecessary to mention the rest that we might recall the "One like unto a jasper and sardine stone" (white light mingled with fire), who sat upon the throne, the four-and-twenty elders who sat upon their thrones, the seven lamps burning before the throne, the four living creatures full of eyes within and without, and that we might remember that heaven is thus pictured to us as a source of illumination for the world. An addition to this picture, which confirms its import, is "the temple of the tabernacle of the *testimony*," which is opened for the purpose of adding to the divine testimony previously given something irresistibly convincing. God has arrows of truth yet in His quiver which He will shoot, to the discomfiture of all His enemies.

What this new and final testimony is is signified by the appearance in heaven of seven angels having the seven last plagues. The term "plague" carries us back to the history of the Israelites in Egypt, and we remember how effectually plagues were used in their behalf against the consolidated power of the world-forces of that age. Imperialism was there, priestcraft was there, sorcery was there, and all that the wisdom of this world could do when inspired by Satanic malice was met, and matched, and broken, by the power of God manifested in judgments. So it is to be at the last; and if now the wild beast of politics, and the dragon of the pit, and the lamb-dragon of an apostate church, with all their allies and emissaries, appear too mighty for us, when God shall make bare His arm the Church of the latter day will triumph, as did that of the earlier.

Yes, this world is to be enlightened; all its mistakes and errors are to be corrected; everybody is to understand the real character of God and the facts of His administration; but this is to be brought about chiefly by the testimony of God concerning Himself. The One like unto a jasper and sardine stone is the spiritual Sun of the universe, and it is because He will continue to shine that the dark places of earth must be lighted up. There must be a change, however, in the character of the light before this purpose can be accomplished. At the era of judgments described in this chapter the red ray of wrath will so predominate as to cause the crystal pavement beneath and before the throne to be shot through and through with fire. In this way is to be explained the fact that now, for the first time among all the references to it in the Scriptures, this sea of glass is said to be "mingled with fire."

All expositors, so far as I have seen, even the best, become incoherent in their attempts to explain this glassy sea. They seem to lose sight of its previous appearances in the record of the divine dealings with men, and fail to interpret it in accordance with those appearances. The effort is to conceive of it as a part of the material scenery of heaven, as if here we had a bit of landscape from Paradise. Interpreters adduce the picture of the closing chapter of the book, where the river, clear as crystal, flows between banks clad in the verdure of the tree of life, as if this, too, were a glimpse of heavenly scenery, and the two must be harmonized with each other. In accordance with this conception the revised version, with the general approval, I think, of expositors, has changed the word *upon*, denoting the situation of the heavenly harpers, to *by*, because, evidently, creatures of flesh and blood like ourselves could not stand *upon* a sea, but only *by* it. The possibility that, in the glorified state, even we may escape from material conditions and be able to stand *on* a sea, as our Lord did, does not seem to have occurred to any one.

But this reminds us again that, in studying this book, we must constantly keep before us the fact that we are not in a literal world, but only in a *world of symbols*. That is a very hard thing to do, but we must do it or be led away into some error. Symbols can stand anywhere, on a sea as well as by it. The question is, What does their standing on it signify more than would be signified by position by it? To answer this question we must get a correct conception of the meaning of the crystal sea. We could omit the interpretation of this symbol in our consideration of the fourth chapter, but now it becomes necessary to understand it.

The first mention of it in the Scriptures is in the twenty-fourth chapter of Exodus, where is described the vision of God by the seventy elders. "They saw the God of Israel: and there was under His feet a *paved work of a sapphire stone*, and as it were *the body of heaven in His clearness.*" The next is in the account of Ezekiel's vision, "The likeness of the *firmament* upon the heads of the living creature was as the color of the *terrible crystal*, and above the *firmament* that was over their heads was the likeness of a throne, as the appearance of a sapphire stone." Now when in the fourth of Revelation we read that "before the throne there was a sea of glass like unto crystal," and then in the fifteenth chapter come to the "sea of glass mingled with fire," we cannot fail to perceive that this sea before the throne is identical with the firmament beneath the throne of the earlier Scriptures. It is the *foundation* of God's *government* at which we are looking, and what is that? Surely not anything material. He does not have to pile up opaque matter to set His throne upon. With Him, supremely, "knowledge is power;" His absolute comprehension of all facts and truths is the necessary basis of His administration. Of that knowledge, that omniscience, the crystal expanse which spreads above our heads is a fitting symbol. He to whom that expanse is as firm as mountain rocks, and who looks through that expanse to behold all lives and all actions, He is the Ruler of the universe.

We are now prepared to understand the sublime position of the saints in this vision. It is a position which speaks of marvellous progress in the understanding of the truth. When last we saw these saints they were with the Lamb, it is true, but upon the earthly elevation of Mount Sion. They were near enough to heaven to hear the heavenly harps, and to catch and learn the new song which floated down to them from the celestial heights. But now where are they? Up above the crystal pavement which supports God's throne, sharing with Him the wide prospect over all His vast domain. They are no longer listening, with bated breath, to catch the distant harmonies and learn them; they are now themselves harpers, and able to take their turn in instructing other pupils. And instead of its being vaguely reported that they are learning a new song, we are now told just what they sing. It is the song of Moses and of the Lamb, saying, "Great and marvellous are Thy works, O Lord God the Almighty; righteous and true are Thy ways, Thou King of the ages."

Now that God's people should come to such superior intelligence by passing into His presence in heaven is a matter of course, and scarcely need be told us by revelation. But that Christian knowledge in this world shall ever reach this stage of enlightenment we should not be able to believe apart from a revelation. Such a revelation we have in this chapter. We must beware of taking it as a picture of the future life, for thus we miss its most important teaching. As in other similar passages of the book, heaven is used as a prophecy of what earth shall yet be.

The description of the heavenly harpers is not to be explained by saying that they are Christians who have died and gone to heaven. Rather are they Christians who have proved superior to all the impostures, and maintained the truth against all the knavery and cruelty of the Devil and his emissaries, and succeeded in putting falsehood and error to flight. Nothing less than this can be meant when it is said that they have "come victorious from the beast, and from his image, and from the number of his name." This must mean, not only that they themselves have been preserved from delusion, but that they have been able to give delusion itself its death-blow. Such is the clearness of their own views of truth, and such their power to convince men of those views, that they may be regarded as standing with God upon the crystal pavement of His throne, and striking the harps from which sound the entrancing harmonies of heaven. They sing the wonderful works and righteous ways of God, and they are permitted to feel that all the nations are to come and worship before Him. They are themselves, in this last great fight of the ages, where Moses and Israel were when the Red Sea closed over their pursuers. These latter-day saints are so happy as to have reached the farther shore of that mighty sea of error which has so long threatened to swallow up all the hopes of the human race.

The parallel between the means by which the Hebrews triumphed and those by which the Church is to gain its final victory is exact. In both cases plagues or judgments accomplish the purpose. In the first case it was ten plagues; here it is seven; but seven is a perfect number, and means all that are necessary. These judgments are executed by angels who come forth from the sanctuary clothed in white raiment, and girded, like the Son of man, with golden girdles, to set forth the conviction of the perfect justice of these visitations which is to prevail upon earth at the time of their coming. Another sign of the same fact is that the seven vials, or bowls, which contain the seven plagues, are presented to the seven angels by one of the four living creatures who are full of eyes, which symbolize the created intelligence of the world. This means that the necessity and justice of these divine judgments are generally understood; they are sent in answer to the demand of all created beings. God will not let fall this last stroke upon human wickedness until all rational beings comprehend its propriety. It will be a stroke which there will be no recalling, against which there will be no interposition; no mediator will strive to arrest it and no saint will pray that it may be averted, for all will feel, above and below, that it is a stroke which ought to fall.

Such a situation is impressively represented by the statement that "the temple was filled with smoke from the glory of God, and from His power; and none was able to enter into the temple till the seven plagues of the seven angels should be finished." When justice, and the necessities of Christ's cause, and the convictions of all intelligent creatures demand judgments, how certain they are to come! The highest attributes of God guarantee them.

XV.

THE SEVEN VIALS.

The sixteenth chapter of the Apocalypse is a description of the judgments, or plagues, by which God will give His truth the victory. If we find it hard to gain distinct conceptions of the details of the symbolism, it may be because we are dealing with a prophecy of events yet future, whose exact nature can never be comprehended until they occur.

One thing, however, is perfectly clear, the terrific completeness of these judgments as a whole upon all forms of error. If one allow his imagination to paint to itself the appearances described in this account of the seven vials, he will find that the globe and all that pertains to it are involved in a catastrophe from which nothing has escaped. It is the world of sinners which has met with such utter disaster; for a time we lose sight entirely of the world of the righteous, who look on and behold the tremendous consequences which persistent wickedness has drawn down upon itself.

Imagine, now, every land of the habitable earth to become the terror-stricken abode of a blighting pestilence in consequence of the pouring out of the contents of the first vial. Let the horrors of the plague in India, or of the cholera in Italy, or of the yellow-fever in our own South, become familiar sights all over the world! Then, at the pouring out of the second vial, let the blue ocean which surrounds the continents become blood red, and let all the living creatures which are in it perish and be cast up upon its shores in putrefying heaps. Then, at the third vial, let the bright streams which rush down the hill-sides, and all the rivers that flow through the lands, be turned into blood, from which the thirsty multitudes turn away with loathing. Then, at the fourth vial, let the sun become so intensified in its fiery energy as to make the world a furnace of torture, and force mankind to burrow in caverns to escape its intolerable rays! Then, at the fifth vial, let the artificial brightness which the wicked have the skill to produce in their dwellings cease to be possible, and let a dreadful darkness, like that of old Egypt, fill all the places of sinful indulgence! Then, at the sixth vial, let the natural barriers, like the Euphrates, which serve to hold in check the angry nations, be removed, and the wild tide of war sweep, unresisted, around the globe! And when men have quarrelled and fought with each other until the spirit of peace can no longer be found anywhere, let the lying emissaries of evil succeed in uniting them in one vast confederacy against God, and bring them in mighty array upon some prodigious battle-field! And then, at the seventh and last vial poured into the air, let the whole circumambient atmosphere burst into flame and explosion, and the heavens above, and the earth beneath, be thrown into convulsions, to swallow up and annihilate all the foes of the Almighty! Such is the picture which Revelation has given us of the final judgments by which God will vindicate His cause and establish His purpose.

It is impossible to imagine any scene, or succession of scenes, more terrible in their appearance or more complete in their devastation.

All this, however, is imagery, sublimely significant, but not for a moment to be literally taken. Worldwide disasters like those portrayed would involve all classes, good and bad, in a common destruction. We must constantly keep in mind that, at that stage of human history which the prophecy has now reached, the Church of God will be in a condition of high prosperity, and truth well on toward its final triumph. The calamities here described will overtake only the persistently ungodly, and *because* their ungodliness is so persistent. It will overtake them in response to the united cry of earth and heaven that such sinners should meet with the fate which their obstinacy has provoked. And their plagues will be all the more awful that they stand in such marked contrast to the happiness and prosperity of the children of God upon the earth. It will be as when the darkness that could be felt reigned over all the land of Egypt, while at the same time light, beautiful light, was in all the dwellings of the Hebrews. The two ways—the way of sin and the way of holiness—will have reached their widest divergence, and those who are in each will learn from the just judgments of God what a difference there is between the "path of the just" and the "way of the transgressor." The judgments themselves, while of a character sufficiently awful to justify the tremendous imagery used to set them forth, must, at the same time, be so far local and personal as to be strictly confined to those who deserve them.

To give a clear and consistent explanation of the objects upon which the seven vials of God's wrath are said to be poured out is more than any one has ever yet done—more, perhaps, than any one can do. Many excellent suggestions have been given, and the trend, both of ancient and modern interpretation, in this part of the Apocalypse, is in harmony with the ideas which have been made prominent in this study of the book. The later commentaries regard the great war of this chapter as a *war of ideas*. But to say just what is meant by the earth, the sea, the fountains, the sun, the throne of the beast, the river Euphrates, and the air, and to make us feel that the explanation is thoroughly consistent with itself and with all the facts to be considered, is a good deal more than any author has yet succeeded in doing, and I frankly confess that I offer my own solution, after much reflection, with great diffidence.

By *the earth* I imagine to be intended that which is most substantial in the arrangements of ungodly society, its organization and civilization, the ties by which it is bound together, and the mutual help by which its parts support each other. This order, though quite selfish in its motive, is yet a great earthly good, and apes, in its appearances and pretensions, the nobler order of the kingdom of heaven. Under its shelter the pleasures and comforts of life find refuge, and make earth, to the unspiritual eye, seem to outrival heaven as a place of abode. At present we see the best results of this earthly order, and men praise civilization at the expense of Christianity. But the time is to come when civilization without Christianity will be seen to be only a hollow shell, a show rather than a substance, and having had time to work out its proper results, it will look as hideous as it really is. The evil at its heart will come to the surface, and make it such a source of trouble and pain that it will have to be cast out of human regard as something leprous.

By *the sea* I would understand the very opposite tendency of human nature to that which binds it together, the tendency to fly asunder in hopeless confusion. This tendency, though springing from precisely the same selfish root as its opposite, is mistaken by many for the very perfection of goodness. Under the names of *freedom* and *independence* it is even worshipped as a kind of god, and men imagine that its possession is heaven upon earth. That which is true only of the nobler liberty of the children of God is attributed to this spurious liberty, which consists really in the freedom to indulge all sinful lusts and passions without restraint. But this wicked sea, whose waters cast up mire and dirt, and whose waves foam out their own shame, is to be revealed by its results in its true character. Socialism and anarchy are to be its bloody fruit until all the world has been taught its vile nature.

By *the rivers* and *fountains of waters* I suppose to be meant the sources of ungodly opinions and the currents of sinful thought to be found in ungodly teaching, whether through the press, institutions of learning, the lecture platform, the heretical pulpit, or any other means of communicating ideas. The vast extent to which false notions are promulgated in various ways, and the confidence which is given to all these deceivers and their deceptions, is one of the most fearful aspects in which a thoughtful mind can view human society. These turbid streams of intellectual corruption which flow through every hamlet and every household appear to the unwise as bright and clear as mountain rivulets, and far more sparkling and refreshing than that river of holy truth, the streams whereof make glad the city of our God. But it will not always be so. The time is to come when false teaching will have produced its results, will have led to the misery which is its legitimate effect, and men will be made to realize that the reading of a bad book, or of a vile newspaper, or the listening to an infidel address, is like having blood to drink.

By *the sun* must be meant the true source of spiritual illumination, God's Word, and the means by which its revelations are made known to men. The Bible ought to be a blessing to every child of our race, but it can be a curse, and must be to those who do not make a good use of it. To a bad man all blessings become curses, and the greatest blessings the worst curses. Getting proof-texts out of the Bible for a false system is a course which must have terrible consequences. And, in the long run, the difference between a reverent study of the Word of God and a frivolous or blasphemous use of it is to show itself in the suffering which will befall the perverse. In the good time coming, when the Scriptures are to be in every human hand, they must either enlighten and comfort with a benignly heightened power, or scorch and blast with a fierceness which shall seem intolerable.

By the *throne of the Beast* is generally understood

the seat of the Papacy, but this seems too narrow a conception to deserve so large a title. No doubt the Papacy belongs to the Beast, but he owns a great deal more and worse. We must remember that in the series of objects mentioned as affected by the blowing of the seven trumpets, a series almost identical with this, the place of the " throne of the beast" is occupied by the " bottomless pit." What can the bottomless pit stand for in this world, but for all that is worst and most diabolical in human life? The beast founds his throne not only upon popish imposture and priestly tyranny, but also upon every species of sin which is found in the world. This throne is wherever men do wickedly with the least hesitation or pretence of something better. It is in the slums, in the saloons, in the brothels, in robbers' row and murderers' alley. In all these places Satan reigns beyond dispute, and they may well be called his kingdom by pre-eminence. This kingdom of night, whose darkness is illuminated chiefly by artificial means, because it abhors the light of day, is destined to be plunged in a midnight from which there shall be no escape.

By *the river Euphrates*, as already intimated, must be meant the natural barriers which fence nations apart, and keep the different sections of the earth from affecting one another. The river Euphrates was, for ages, the obstruction which kept the human hive to the east of it from swarming over on to the Western nations. No man can realize the unspeakable benefit to the Western peoples from being thus shut away from the evils which had grown gigantic in their long-time dwelling-place. But the tendency of modern civilization is to throw down all barriers between nations, and to cause them to meet and mingle in a common life. The pursuit of gain or of other selfish objects sets the current of humanity to moving all round the world. The result of this intermingling, to those who have no safeguard against it, must be pernicious. All merely conventional morality, all superficial virtue, all only formal religion, must perish in this process. Every kingdom, except the kingdom of heaven, will be so shaken as to disclose the worthlessness of its foundations.

What can be meant by *the air* upon which the seventh vial is poured? It must be something as all-inclusive as the atmosphere. It must be something as vital as the breath. I can think of nothing which fulfils these conditions except God Himself. I remember that the "wind which bloweth where it listeth" is the symbol of the Holy Spirit, and that we are said to "live, and move, and have our being" in God. This is true of the wicked as well as of the righteous. They are as truly in God as they are in the atmosphere. The kingdom of evil is surrounded on every side by Him who includes all things in Himself. The fatal fact about all the dark empire of the Devil is that it is in contact everywhere with the Blessed One. Minor calamities can spring from the misuse of subordinate good, but when God Himself becomes a curse to His creatures, how great the curse must be! If the manifold relationship of men to God turns against them, it will be as if the whole atmosphere about the earth became an inflammable gas, and a spark touched it all into explosion.

These seven plagues, like those of Egypt, are to be regarded partly as natural results and partly as tremendous aggravations of those results by the divine fiat. The pouring out of the vials, or bowls, indicates a positive exertion of divine power in the way of punishment.

The effects of these plagues upon the minds of the human race I suppose to be indicated at three points in the narrative: after the third vial, after the sixth, and after the seventh. The student of sacred numbers may, perhaps, see design and art in this arrangement. There is certainly a method in the plan by which, at the close of the third judgment, we are shown the effect of the divine action upon God's people, at the close of the sixth plague the effect upon the still unregenerate, and finally, after the seventh, the grand cumulative result upon the entire world.

Is it not what we should expect, that the ready docility of God's people would learn the great lesson before half of the series had been completed? We are not surprised, then, after the description of the turning of the rivers and fountains into blood, to hear the angel of the waters say: "Thou art righteous, O Lord, which art, and wast, and shalt be, because Thou hast judged thus. For they have shed the blood of saints and prophets, and Thou hast given them blood to drink: for they are worthy." The sense of justice thus expressed is heightened by comparing that justice, first, with the rectitude of the divine nature, and, secondly, with the atrocious wickedness of the ungodly. Then a voice responds out of the altar, "Even so, Lord God Almighty, true and righteous are Thy judgments."

These words of satisfaction we may trace to those souls under the altar who, in the account of the fifth seal (6 : 10), were crying so earnestly for vengeance upon their murderers. We may take both of these utterances—that of the angel of the waters and the response from the altar—as the expression of the thorough conviction and hearty acknowledgment of the Church of the latter day of the spotless holiness of God, and His perfect justice in dealing with the human race. We believe in both these facts, but we have not had the perfect demonstration of them which the future history of the world is to furnish to the Church.

On the other hand, how much a matter of course it is to find that, even after the sixth plague, the unregenerate portion of mankind are still apparently as far from learning their lesson as ever! We are reminded of Pharaoh's behavior, and how, after the ninth plague, he hardened his heart in utter madness of obstinacy, and forbade Moses to see his face again on penalty of death. So it always is, so it always must be, with that unteachable perversity of spirit which, though ever learning, never comes to the knowledge of the truth. Accordingly, in the days of the last plagues, the greatest frenzy of opposition which the world has seen is represented as breaking out only just before that final stroke by which the Almighty is to crush all resistance.

This last and greatest effort prior to the millennium, to prevent the setting up of the divine kingdom upon earth, is described as incited by three frog-like, unclean spirits, issuing from the mouths of the dragon, the beast, and the false prophet. These devilish spirits, by means of lying miracles wrought in the presence of the kings of the earth, succeed in uniting them in one tremendous conspiracy, and gathering them in multitudinous array to the great war against God Almighty. So gigantic are to be the last throes of error in its desperate struggle to maintain its footing upon the earth. The Devil, the demagogue, and the sophist will keep up their bad arts to the "last ditch" of their ability. Lying, and misrepresentation, and calumny are not to retire from the field until forced from it. The blessed truth of God will win its final triumph not by any concession or favor of its opposers, but by sheer weight of metal and force of arm to annihilate resistance.

And thus it is represented as taking place in the last act of the drama. When the seventh vial is poured out upon the air, and the whole spiritual envelope of the world bursts into explosion, the convulsions which follow are so universal and so profound as to put an end to all opposition. Thus, on the night of the destruction of the first-born, Egyptian gainsaying ended for a time in urgent entreaties that the Hebrews would do the very thing which they had long been forbidden to do. A voice is heard, like that which came from the cross, saying, "It is finished!" Finished we must suppose will be all denial of Gospel truth, all resistance to Gospel methods. A spiritual revolution, the greatest that has ever been seen upon earth, will then take place. How great must it be to be pictured by a world-wide thunder-storm, a universal earthquake, the cleaving of the great city of the earth— that is, the combined organization and civilization of mankind—into three parts, the fall of all the cities, as Jericho fell before Joshua, and the entire transformation of the earth's surface, so that every island fled away and every mountain disappeared! Add to this scene the awful hail, every stone of the weight of a talent (about fifty pounds), and what opposition could any longer live to raise its hand against the Almighty? The meaning of the prophecy is clear and hopeful; it is within God's power to put an end to all resistance to His truth and His cause, and end it He surely will. There shall come a time when the Gospel will no longer find an opposer to raise a doubt of its truth, or to suggest delay in accepting its invitations. What a time for the Church that will be! Who that thinks of it can fail to pray, " Thy kingdom come"!

XVI.

THE SCARLET WOMAN.

No intelligent Christian can read the seventeenth and eighteenth chapters of the Apocalypse understandingly without having his heart leap within him at the things there set forth. For there can be no doubt, there *is* no doubt, in the minds of all qualified interpreters, that we are here assured of the downfall of all those systems of counterfeit Christianity of which Romanism is the most formidable instance. The description of these spurious systems, and of their final and awful overthrow, is the subject of these two chapters of the prophecy.

But what prophecy it was, and how thoroughly and joyously we may recognize it as such, which, centuries before the rise of the Romish apostasy, and eighteen hundred years before some of the events which are now fulfilling some of the predictions, so distinctly and graphically portrayed the principal features of the whole miserable history! We can well believe in the final catastrophe so emphatically promised, when we perceive that the prescience which assures us of it foresaw so much else which is already a matter of history, but which anything less than omniscience would have been equally unable to discover.

How little idea, apart from a divine revelation, a mere mortal like John could have had, in the first century of the Christian era, that the most formidable antagonist which the religion of Christ was to have would be a pretender to be that very religion ! And if conjecture had reached even so far as to forecast such a prodigy, how far it must have fallen short of any detailed description of the exact features of the prodigy, and of its special fortunes ! Yet John did, by inspiration, see just what Roman Catholicism and its kindred errors would be, what would be the main elements of their impostures, what the awful extent of the evil which they would work, and also, thank God ! what would be the causes of their downfall and the joy over their destruction. All these facts are set forth so plainly that he who runs may read them and take courage that, although the end has not yet come, it is sure to come in God's appointed time.

Of course there are those who are determined not to see what is here revealed, if they can avoid doing so. There are two classes of persons who are not willing to read these chapters with their eyes open. Romanists are not willing to see in this harlot their own beloved Church, and rationalists are not willing to find so remarkable an evidence of inspiration as such a prophecy must be admitted to furnish. But the very efforts which these two classes have made to avoid these conclusions only serve to show, to unprejudiced minds, that the prophecy is clear and beyond reasonable cavil. Both Romanists and rationalists admit that the subject of these chapters must be *Rome*. Rome is so distinctly pointed out as to give no chance for doubt that it is intended. The admission is fatal to these objectors ; for the details of the vision cannot be made to fit anything but *papal* Rome, and the endeavor of Bossuet to make them fit *imperial* Rome, or that of Renan to make the story of Nero's reputed survival and reappearance explain the profound expression "the beast that was, and is not, and shall come," are both so puerile as to show that only one interpretation is possible.

The fact that the information contained in the seventeenth chapter is derived from one of the angels who had the seven vials, or bowls, of judgment, shows that this is a special episode of the era of judgments, which is now, on account of its great importance, more particularly described. How important it is! Who can fail to realize the tremendous obstacle to the world's enlightenment which the Papacy and its sister delusions are? Which of us has not sometimes staggered, like Macaulay, at the spectacle of its imposing power, and trembled lest that power should last as long as the world stands? If we do not, with Macaulay, think it probable that Romanism may continue in perennial freshness and vigor "when some traveller from New Zealand shall, in the midst of a vast solitude, take his stand on a broken arch of London Bridge to sketch the ruins of St. Paul's," it is because, unlike the English historian, we believe that we have here an inspired prediction of its utter disappearance from the world, a prediction in which we have more confidence than in the conclusions of our own short-sighted understandings.

The Papacy is here described by symbols which show her to be the most formidable adversary which God's truth and cause could possibly have. She is the *harlot*, false to God, while pretending to be true and faithful to Him as her husband. She succeeds in passing herself off for the true Church, while the Church itself is suffering in the wilderness. She sits upon a scarlet-colored beast which is at once the red-dragon, the Devil, and the wild beast of worldly empire. All that Satan can do to sustain her, and all that the unscrupulous spirit of political power can do, will be done. Fraud and misrepresentation she carries to an extent unknown before, for whereas the wild beast of worldly empire had names of blasphemy only upon his heads, this vision of imposture is *full* of names of blasphemy. The rich dress of the harlot and the golden cup in her hand betoken the use of the power of money to an almost unlimited extent. The result of this awful combination of unholy forces is represented to be the debauching of the kings of the earth, and the turning mankind at large into a mob of spiritual drunkards. What could be more dreadful, as a religious state, than one fit to be represented by a condition of general intoxication? And the worst thing about drunkenness is its tendency to perpetuate itself, the present degradation ensuring its own continuance by producing an insatiable craving for its cause.

For between one and two thousand years these sad predictions have been fulfilled in the history of Romanism and in that of its sister harlot, the so-called Eastern Church. Through this protracted period the many millions of devotees of these false systems have been deceived into believing that they belonged to the only true Church, and were, therefore, sure of salvation. The imposture is still kept up with such success that the real Church and the actual way of salvation are discredited by hundreds of millions of people, and it seems as if the fraud were destined to be perpetual. Although the real character of the scarlet woman has shown itself again and again, although she has been proved a liar a thousand times, and her savage thirst for the blood of the saints has opened the eyes of a great many, yet nevertheless she keeps up her effrontery from century to century, and finds "peoples, and multitudes, and nations, and tongues" to believe in her.

It was most natural that the apostle "wondered with a great wonder" as he contemplated this prodigious phenomenon. It is not strange that the ignorant masses of the adherents of these gigantic frauds are beguiled and bewitched by the vast display of authority and glory which these false churches are able to make. That the cunning of man, even when assisted by the guile of the serpent, should be able to achieve such marvels as to pass off the false church for the true, and Antichrist for Christ; that priestcraft should reach the height of vaulting to the seat of empire, and of putting a hierarchy of its own creation, which, at the time of the prophecy, was not yet born, upon the throne of the world, so that it should become the eighth head of the great political monster under whose feet mankind had so long groaned; that a selfish earthly dynasty, seeking chiefly its own power and glory at the expense of others, should be shrewd and subtle enough to bend to its own purposes the ten other kings as selfish as itself, so that for ages they should give their power and authority to the beast—all this is matter of marvel so great as to surpass all other similar occasions of wonder that the world has seen. In the success and perpetuity of the Roman apostasy the author of evil has achieved his masterpiece.

We are not, however, to think that this masterpiece of iniquity is forever to flaunt its blasphemous pretensions in the faces of an outraged Church and an indignant Heaven. It is all the more surely doomed that its exceptional enormity challenges God and all good beings to seek its destruction. Singled out, as it is, on account of its large share in the ruin of mankind, for express mention and description in the Apocalypse, it is its awful part in the era of judgments for which chiefly it has a place there. The history of its perverse career, though so protracted, is given most briefly, but the account of its fall is given extensively and dramatically. After all, it is the overthrow of this gigantic evil, and not its long-continued existence, of which the Book of Revelation takes most solemn heed.

The first warning of this overthrow is in the statement that this nondescript monster, which is sometimes the woman, sometimes the beast, and sometimes the great city seated upon its seven hills and reigning over the kings of the earth, makes war, through these kings, *against the Lamb*. The Lamb of the Apocalypse is the very One whose task it is to unseal the great book of the divine knowledge, so that human ignorance shall be enlightened. The Romish Church has set itself with all the force of its authority and all the power of its worldly alliances to resist that unsealing. Which is to prevail? "The Lamb shall overcome them, for He is Lord of lords and King of kings." The Pope is only the ruler of the kings of the earth, but Christ is the Lord of the kings of the universe. What abundant resources He has at His disposal to give Him the victory in this battle of the light with the darkness every morning proclaims. There is the same superabundant degree of truth to be kept out of human minds in order to preserve the darkness of paganism and of popery, that there is of light to be kept out of the world to preserve the darkness of the night.

"They also shall overcome that are with Him, called, and chosen, and faithful." They must overcome by the very fact that they are *with Him*. His victory is their victory. The cause for which they are ready to die, until the apostate church is "drunk with the blood of the saints, and with the blood of the martyrs of Jesus," is, of necessity, the winning cause. The testimony which they bear who are "called, and chosen, and faithful," both by their lives and by their lips, is testimony which must eventually convince every gainsayer that the scarlet woman is anything but the bride of Christ.

Then there is an element of natural, reactionary retribution, which has a part in the judgment of that brazen harlot, the church which aims at temporal dominion through alliances with the civil power. Earthly princes are like dogs fighting for the same bone, and any ecclesiasticism which succeeds in using the civil power for political ends is sure to suffer, sooner or later, from the jealousy and hatred of that same power. All State churches have their sore troubles from this cause, and the Romish Church, because it is the most flagrant example of this abuse, is destined to suffer most severely its natural consequences. The "ten kings" who before gave their "power and authority unto the beast" are afterward seen hating the harlot, and making her desolate, and naked, and eating her flesh, and burning her utterly with fire. The beast itself, on which she once rode, turns against her, and heads the confederacy of the hostile kings. This is a natural consequence of the lust for power which all worldly empires share with the Church of Rome. They succumbed to her as long as she could frighten them into submission through their superstitious terrors, or play them one against another by her superior craft. But with the dawn of popular knowledge her opportunity passed, and already, among her former royal serfs, there is none so poor as to do her reverence. They have done much to make her uncomfortable, they have taken from her every vestige of temporal power. The "prisoner of the Vatican" is having a sorry time of it in keeping up a poor show of temporal sovereignty. It certainly looks far from improbable that the political changes of Europe may yet work as utter a wreck of the Papacy as is pictured in this prophecy.

XVII.

THE FALL OF BABYLON.

The downfall of the apostate church is portrayed in the eighteenth chapter. For the purpose of such a portrayal the figure of a woman is exchanged for that of a great city, because thus the disaster could be made so much more dramatic. Inspiration seems to have wished to enlarge upon this downfall, to paint it in such dark colors as to cause the readers of the prophecy to feel how great an event this is to God as well as to us. The overthrow of Rome and of its kindred systems will mark one of the grandest eras in human history.

We are not left to think that for so great a service to God and man we are to be indebted chiefly to the selfish and beastly spirit of worldly empire. That will have its part to do, as set forth in the seventeenth chapter, but it will be a very subordinate part. Rome will fall, not so much because its worldly possessions excite the envy of covetous spirits like its own, as because the world will become too bright a place for such a creature of darkness longer to lurk in.

For again, at the outset of this dramatic description of the fall of mystic Babylon, as so often before in the Revelation, we meet the now familiar symbol of human enlightenment. Not in the elaborate descriptions of earlier chapters, for that is unnecessary, but sufficiently indicated to remind us that here as elsewhere the book is the account of the manner in which the truth of heaven is to displace the error of earth. In this simple manner is to be explained the meaning of the appearance of an "angel coming down out of heaven with great authority," with whose glory "the earth was lightened."

Recall the statement that the victory of the Lamb is to be that of those who are "with Him, who are called, and chosen, and faithful." Remember that Jesus ere He ascended spoke of the *authority* that had been given Him in heaven and upon earth, and bade His disciples go upon their mission, counting upon Him to be with them alway, even unto the end of the world. What is this accession of authority, then, which comes to earth with the angel, but the authority of Jesus exercised by His true people in increased measure? It is the authority of goodness, of righteousness, and of truth over an ever-augmenting population. It is "the kingdom, and dominion, and the greatness of the kingdom under the whole heaven," which Daniel foretold should be "given to the people of the saints of the Most High." The right side in this great world battle is here seen obtaining a decidedly predominant influence over men. As they learn to defer to the true Church, the false church will lose its power. As the authority of Jesus increases over mankind, the dominion of the spiritual despotisms will diminish. This angel was so splendid that "the earth was lightened with his glory." Let the imagination see something far beyond a temporary illumination, like that which lit up the fields of Bethlehem and touched every object within the horizon with a brief brilliancy. The fact intended is unspeakably greater than such a conception. It is the fact of the prevalence of such intelligence in the world, such knowledge of the ways of God and of the truths of the Bible, such power to discriminate between the true Church of Christ and any possible counterfeits, that *no place is left anywhere* for popery to live, and it can have no choice but to die.

Such a thought about earth is almost enough to take one's breath away. But is it any more than is implied by the angel when he cries, "*Fallen, fallen is Babylon the great*"? Babylon will never fall, I am sure, until all the supports on which it rests are removed. As long as there are foolish, ignorant, superstitious people in the world, so long popery and its fellow-impostures will take advantage of those people and maintain their existence. They can be destroyed only by removing the very ground from beneath their feet and the very breath from their nostrils. This can be done only by increasing the general enlightenment to such a degree that the weaknesses, and mistakes, and vices on which Rome lives shall disappear from the earth. Let men everywhere learn the facts of history, the facts of the Bible, and the facts of human nature, and great Babylon must then have its fall.

The first step toward the emancipation of the race from the thraldom of great spiritual despotisms is the discovery of their inherent vileness. When Tetzel came peddling indulgences through Germany, and when Luther went to Rome and found that the very priests who transubstantiated the wafers into God were infidels who secretly ridiculed the whole performance, it became hard to remain a Romanist. We are to anticipate like discoveries everywhere, and the fair mask to be so completely torn from the face of the papacy that its ugliness will be universally seen. It will be as if a glorious angel had proclaimed in every human ear that Babylon the great "*is a habitation of demons, and a hold of every unclean spirit, and a hold of every unclean and hateful bird.*" The Protestant Church has long been saying that, but Catholics would not believe it. The time will come when they will have to believe it, because the exposure of papal iniquity will be so complete. Popish influence will not always be able to falsify history or to keep the true record of the apostate church out of the common schools and from the knowledge of the people. It will finally be known how the kings of the earth have committed fornication with this spiritual harlot, and what they have had to suffer in consequence. It will be seen how poor old Spain and every other Catholic country has gone down under the incubus of its idolatrous faith, and how every Protestant country has risen by the inspiration of its purer faith. It will be seen how the masses of the people, wherever Romanism has prevailed, have grovelled in a degradation like that of sots under the power of inebriation. It will be known how large a part of her support Rome derives from the panders to her illicit pleasures and from the favorites with whom she shares the spoils which have been plucked from the unhappy victims of her power. When these things are laid bare and spread out before the world in all their revolting deformity, popery must go the way of all criminals—into disgrace and punishment.

Then will be heard another voice from heaven, saying, "Come forth, My people, out of her, that ye have no fellowship with her sins, and that ye receive not of her plagues. For her sins have reached even unto heaven, and God hath remembered her iniquities." Interpreters who take the symbolism of this chapter literally, or semi-literally, are perplexed to tell whose this other voice is, whether God's or another angel's. But if we take these heavenly occurrences for what is to transpire upon earth, there is instant suggestion how this voice speaks. It is the response arising within the apostate church itself upon hearing and understanding the facts uttered by the angel of exposure—that is, as the testimony of God's people becomes strong and convincing regarding the hideous character of the false church, there will arise a cry within the communion of that church for separation from her. It is conceivable that real piety may remain in the midst of spurious religious bodies as long as their real character continues concealed in the least degree. But when their hypocrisy is unmasked, it is as impossible for true Christians to abide with them as it would be for lambs to rest in the embrace of wolves. Sooner or later all that is good will have left these synagogues of Satan, and nothing will remain that is not entirely Satanic.

It may well be imagined that the loudest and severest denunciations will be heard from these who are the latest outcomers from the apostasies. The horror of having continued in such bad company so long, and of having been so shockingly ensnared and beguiled, will cause the sharpest indignation. These last separatists will be the most familiar with the atrocities which they denounce, and most thoroughly aware of all their damnable ill-desert. Accordingly it is from these that the cry is represented as going up to God for His heavy vengeance upon the harlot city. "Render unto her even as she rendered, and double unto her the double according to her works: in the cup that she mingled, mingle unto her double." These recusants who, perhaps, have been suffered to remain in the communion of devils for this very purpose, are represented as bearing witness against it regarding its self-glorification, and wantonness, and confidence of unlimited indulgence. And it is these who are to see with clearest vision the utter ruin with which the just judgment of God will overtake this greatest enemy of righteousness on earth.

But others still are to see it. Not only the last generation of Puritans and Protestants who go forth from the apostate church, but those whose spiritual sight is far less keen. Even the "kings of the earth, who committed fornication and lived wantonly with her," and are therefore no better than herself, are yet to be fully able to see the judgment upon her, and to fear lest they themselves may be involved in it. Moreover, the "merchants of the earth," that class of men who worship money and are eager for any traffic, even in the "souls of men," if they can but see a chance for gain, even these are shown as being fully aware of and lamenting over the catastrophe of the great, vile city. And finally, the "shipmasters" and "mariners," men whose calling is supposed to make them rather more ignorant and unscrupulous than any other class, are pictured as standing "afar off," and bewailing the smoke of the burning metropolis. This vivid picture of a great city in conflagration, beheld by horrified spectators of these various kinds, seems intended to assure us that the final downfall of great hypocrisies will be understood by all mankind. The light will have become so general and so bright that, at that time, nobody will be so ignorant and foolish as great numbers are now. Even into the marts of trade, even into the cabinets of civil rulers, the great truths of religion, the great principles of righteousness will have penetrated, so that even the most ungodly will fear to deceive and take advantage, as Romanism has done, lest they, too, should partake of her Heaven-sent judgments.

When that day has arrived, what a change will have come over all the relations of human intercourse! Christianity has no harder task before her than to reform politics and commerce. In both the spirit of an almost unbridled license reigns, and all means are unhesitatingly used which promise a wicked success. But in the day that the world becomes too intelligent and too clean for the pope and his cardinals to dwell in it, the politician and the merchant will have to mend their ways. The tricks of trade and the wiles of diplomacy will have to be abandoned. Selfishness may yet survive, but it will have to be decent and respectable. This will be a vastly better world.

The best of all will be that the ogres, once banished, are never to come back again. The last act in this drama is most assuring. A strong angel takes up a great stone like a mill-stone (fit emblem of the nature of superstition) and casts it into the sea, saying, "Thus . . . Babylon . . . shall be found no more at all." The disappearance of the stone illustrates the disappearance of popery from the world. It was here—it is gone—it will never be seen again. Oh, blessed time, when men shall tell their children of mighty systems of priestcraft which once numbered their victims by hundreds of millions, and the children shall find it hard to believe the strange story, because nothing is anywhere to be found upon the earth to make it seem possible! How near that age will be to what we are accustomed to think of as the millennium!

XVIII.

THE PREMILLENNIAL AGE.

We have not yet quite reached the golden age of the Church, but the prophecy is rapidly hastening toward it. The good already described as secured is so great as to seem little short of millennial glory. However, a few steps yet remain to be taken before we shall be face to face with that glory. But each one of these steps is itself so delightful that they seem like the latter part of "the path of the just" where it becomes "the perfect day."

The first thing in the nineteenth chapter is just what we might anticipate. When priestcraft shall disappear forever from the earth, sinking like a millstone into the depths of the sea, will there not be a great celebration? We can almost hear the shouts of that celebration as they reverberate from heaven to earth, and through creation's utmost bounds. Wherever Jesus is known and honored, and wherever tidings of earthly occurrences extend, there will there be rejoicing when it is known that the dark system of imposture which so long wore the livery of heaven in the service of Satan has ceased to be possible upon this planet. Priestcraft will last too long ever to be forgotten by mankind; its extent will be too great and its mischief too vast to permit it ever to pass from human memory, so that its "smoke will go up forever and ever" as a hideous recollection.

All the more jubilant and prolonged will be the celebration of the fall of this mighty Babylon that its career was so protracted. The description represents "a great multitude in heaven" crying "Hallelujah!" And a second time they say "Hallelujah!" The "four-and-twenty elders" who represent the Church of all ages, and the "four living creatures" in whom is personified universal intelligence, "fall down and worship God" and cry "Hallelujah!" A voice comes from the throne saying, "Give praise to our God!" And finally "a voice of a great multitude, and as the voice of many waters, and as the voice of mighty thunders," is heard saying "Hallelujah! for the Lord our God, the Almighty, reigneth."

What less can be meant by all this than a general recognition by all mankind of the hand of God in the overthrow of all systems of priestcraft, and a general rejoicing at it? We are to understand that popery and kindred impostures come to an end by the universal desire of mankind and to the general satisfaction; and that it is to take place upon high moral and religious grounds—grounds which men generally will have sufficient moral and religious education to perceive.

It has been thought that the use here, for the first and only time in the New Testament, of the Hebrew term "Hallelujah" is a hint that at this point the *conversion of the Jews* will take place. It is a suggestion which seems highly probable. Otherwise we have no hint in this book of that event from which, in the eleventh of Romans, Paul expected so much. "What shall the receiving of them be," he asks, "but life from the dead?" Was not his prophetic eye upon the same millennial fact which, in the next chapter of the Apocalypse, is termed "the first resurrection"? It is most probable. We ought to be looking in our prophetic history for the conversion of the Jews somewhere here. And is it not extremely likely that the light which proves too bright for Romanism will be too bright for Judaism also? How can Jewish Rabbis continue to terrorize their adherents in a world where Romish priests have lost their power? Indeed, Judaism is, and always has been, one of the worst forms of priestcraft, and when one form goes all must go, and for the same reason. We may well suppose that, among the liberated millions who rejoice over the downfall of these old world tyrannies, it will be the Jews who will rejoice most loudly. It may well be that the Hebrew Hallelujah will rise highest among all the notes of praise, because, of all the victims of spiritual despotisms, it is the Jews whose curse has been most awful. Was it not the malignity of Jewish priestcraft which murdered the Lord and brought His blood upon that race for many generations?

There must be at this same time not only the conversion of the Jews, but a general revival of religion. What can prevent it? With those great hindrances out of the way whose destruction has been already described, how great the power of the preached gospel must become! And now another great and wonderful help to its influence is brought to view under the figure of the *marriage of the Lamb* to the bride, the Church. The same multitudinous voice which thundered Hallelujah is heard saying that "the marriage of the Lamb is come, and *His wife hath made herself ready.*" The narrative continues, "And it was given unto her that she should array herself in fine linen, bright and pure; for the fine linen is the righteousness of the saints."

Others may think that they have here a warrant for expecting the personal advent of the Lord Jesus at this epoch. Such is not my opinion. I think that if that were meant, more emphasis would be put upon the personal appearance of the *Bridegroom.* As it is the emphasis is upon the bride, and her fitness for the long-delayed nuptials. In the line of the view which we have been taking this description brings before us the greatly increased honor and confidence which the Church is to receive in the age which we are considering. When the false church goes down, the true Church must go up. When her rivals in human regard are discredited, the real bride of Christ will be admired as she deserves to be. The Church will deserve admiration at this period because of its righteousness; it will be clothed, like a bride, in spotless white. When the preaching of the gospel is sustained by such a church, what conquests it will win! Not only in heaven, but upon earth it will be said, "Blessed are they who are bidden to the marriage supper of the Lamb!" All over the world the gospel invitation will be joyfully accepted, and the wedding will be furnished with guests. It will be the greatest revival ever known.

It is not strange that at this point John was so moved by what had been shown him that he fell at the feet of the angel through whom the communication had come to worship him. If we realize with any vividness the picture of that glad time, we too shall feel like worship. The angel restrained the apostle with the assurance that he was no better than any other angel, or indeed any other servant of God, though it was his happy lot to bring so glorious a message. The incident may stand for the heightened spirit of worship which shall pervade the Church in the premillennial age.

What next? Is this state of things, which the marriage supper of the Lamb represents, to go on without interruption or opposition? Is the history of the Church now to be only one continued and everywhere spreading revival of religion? Or shall we look for reaction, reverses, and some great combination against the truth and against the Church?

Remember that, although we have seen the downfall of the apostate church, some other notable figures of this prophecy remain yet upon the stage of action. There are yet the wild beast of worldly power and the false prophet of deceit, who inherits the wily spirit of the lamb-dragon of ecclesiasticism; above all, there is Satan, the red dragon and master-spirit of evil; and all these have the same capacity for opposition that they ever had, all the more embittered because of the great progress and power of true religion. It is in the very nature of things, then, that there should be one more great spiritual war upon the earth before it can have its millennium.

This war succeeds the marriage supper. There was never a revival, I suppose, that did not stir up enmity among the ungodly. So it will be in the last days, and on a vast scale. The powers of darkness will not see their empire slipping from them without a desperate effort to recover it. It will be a great struggle, ending with a complete and tremendous discomfiture.

It is to be supposed that, even with the largely diffused knowledge, both secular and religious, which must by this time everywhere prevail, and notwithstanding the fact that priestcraft has disappeared and that the Church enjoys an unrivalled pre-eminence, there will yet be many unregenerate persons in the world whose carnal minds will be hostile to God. It is among these, through all social grades, from bottom to top, that Satan and his emissaries will work their plot and organize their confederacy. Whatever doubt can be raised in an unbelieving mind, whatever dislike can be fostered in a corrupt heart, whatever tools can be found in selfish, proud, or malignant natures—these elements of discord and opposition to God Satan will strive to turn to account as long as the world is not entirely sanctified, and he is free to scheme and act.

The result of such a conflict in the age just before the millennial is easily predicted. All the victories of the Church in less enlightened ages forecast its overwhelming success in this last struggle. How can it fail? Its forces are pictured in the passage before us as a magnificent heavenly army all upon white horses, and led by the great Captain of salvation Himself. The largest part of the description is that of the

Leader. Of the led we are told only that they are clothed in fine linen, white and pure. But of the Leader the portrait is given in many striking details. His names, His armor, His diadems, His clothing are all described minutely. The result is to make us feel how splendidly equipped the Church of the latter day will be for its last great campaign. It will be strong in its own purity, strong in the authority of the Word of God in an age sufficiently intelligent to appreciate the claims and the evidences of Inspiration, strongest of all in its manifest favor with Him who is King of kings and Lord of lords, and in the enlarged knowledge of Him for which the premillennial age will be distinguished.

This I take to be the significance of that splendid figure, the rider upon a white horse, who heads the grand army of Christianity for its great war with the forces of evil. Few, if any, would venture to say that this means the personal advent of the Lord Jesus. If not that, it must mean a vastly heightened knowledge of His person and character, which is equivalent for the practical purpose in view to such an advent. Is not such a knowledge precisely what we may anticipate as existing in the premillennial age? The progress of the world's improvement already described could never have gone so far without such a knowledge, and each step of that progress must add to the world's acquaintance with the Lord. At the point which we have now reached the information prevailing everywhere regarding King Jesus must be considered the most important and most hopeful fact of the earthly situation.

Carefully examine the description of the divine General, and you will be impressed that its principal item is the *names* of the great Personage seen: (1) He is "called Faithful and True." (2) "He hath a name written which no one knoweth but He Himself." (3) "His name is called the Word of God." (4) "He hath on His garment and on His thigh a name written, King of kings and Lord of lords." Names are knowledge. They are descriptions of character and summaries of history. Titles are acquired by great deeds and remarkable careers. We cannot be mistaken in regarding this recital of the titles of Jesus, as He appears at the head of His hosts, as the expression of the knowledge of Him that is to prevail in the world in the age which we are now considering. Like a field-marshal at the head of his troops, He is seen covered with decorations, every one of which tells of some grand exploit or of some honorable promotion.

A general thus renowned marches to certain triumph. His mere name strikes consternation into the breasts of His enemies. History tells how the name of Lord Clive once scattered an army in India; the report of his approach dissolved the force which had been gathered to meet him. It is surely not too much to expect that when, for the last time before the millennium, the ungodly gather for a great crusade against Christianity, the name of Christ, with all its accumulated glory, will carry consternation to the hearts of that confederation. His well-known faithfulness to His people through so many ages, the demonstrated truth of both His promises and His threatenings, the fact that He so far transcends all statement or description, that He is the revelation of God, and that so many of earth's most kingly kings have acknowledged His sovereignty—all these facts will be so inseparably associated with His name that that name alone will carry victory with it in its mere utterance.

The completeness of the conquest is set forth in several astonishing particulars. The one most immediately impressive is the carnage to which an angel, standing in the sun, invites all the scavenger birds of the solar system. It will be such an overthrow as took place at one of those great battles of history, where the course of empire was permanently changed by a most sanguinary slaughter. At Chalons, where Theodoric and his Romans checked the impetuous advance of Attila and the Huns, it was said by some that one hundred and sixty-two thousand, by others that three hundred thousand were left dead on the field. Such a complete rout we are to understand the Church to inflict upon all its opponents. But we must remember that the character of that rout is spiritual rather than carnal. The standing-place of the angel who proclaims it must be thought of not as the literal sun, but as the great source of truth and knowledge. The sword of the great Commander, which goes out of His mouth, is not a sword of steel, but of intellectual and moral illumination. The victory will be that grandest of all victories, when opponents cease to be such not by being deprived of bodily life, but by being convinced of the unrighteousness of their cause, and enemies not only cease to be enemies, but become true and ardent friends. Such is the sublime triumph which the lofty character of Jesus and His magnificent history invite us to expect in the days when He shall have carried His cause and His people to the very verge of millennial glory. We could not be satisfied with anything less—surely not with a horrible triumph of physical force, such as a literal interpretation of this passage would find in it.

But the real nature of this success is made still more certain by the statement that it includes the capture and destruction of the beast and the false prophet. We are brought face to face with the actual end of the world-power, of all that political system which rests on fraud and violence rather than on righteousness and truth. The world has been so long ruled by unscrupulous ambition and greed that anything different and superior in politics seems almost as unattainable as heaven. But the time is to come, it is here shown as if already arrived, when human government is to cease to be administered on selfish principles, and all its laws and institutions are to be brought into agreement with the Bible and the Church.

Not only the world-power, but the false prophet is to be destroyed. This is the greatest victory of all. When popery and priestcraft perished false teaching survived. The priests are only one class of the blind guides. Every infidel propagandist, every sophistical newspaper, every bad book, all kinds of liars and all kinds of lies must be regarded as included in the false prophet. When he ends they end. Will it not be wonderful? Think of a world so bright with learning, so filled with the knowledge of the Lord, so universally educated and informed that no lie has any longer any chance of being believed! It seems too much ever to be true. But it is not too much, for "the mouth of the Lord hath spoken it."

XIX.

THE MILLENNIUM.

He who has kept company with me through the Apocalyptic scenes of the preceding chapter has probably felt that the condition of the world there described was such as to admit little further improvement. We are, indeed, well on toward the consummation of the prophetic drama; long ago mere human imagination would have failed to invent any new notes of progress; but the invention of inspiration, with the divine foreknowledge for its basis, has yet some steps to take before reaching its conclusion.

The twentieth chapter of Revelation opens with an account of the binding of Satan by an angel who comes down out of heaven, having the key of the abyss and a great chain in his hand. He lays hold of Satan and binds him and casts him into the abyss and shuts and seals it for a thousand years, during which the devil can no more deceive the nations.

Alford is sure that this is a veritable angel who binds Satan, but the reader may be asked to reflect if what has already been described be not the actual process of putting the Adversary in fetters? Is not Satan restricted by every advance of the truth, every success of the Church, every defeat of his minions? The spread of knowledge which renders priestcraft henceforth impossible, does not that fetter the Devil?

The prevalence of correct political ideas, does not that mightily hinder the Archdemon? The education of the race up to the point where false prophets and deceivers of every kind lose their occupation; how can the father of lies ply his trade after that? It is evident that the history given in the nineteenth chapter was really a process of binding Satan, so that the grand angel, with his key and chain, has little more to do than to picture to our minds what has already virtually come to pass. He serves to remind us that the progress of spiritual enlightenment is essentially heavenly in its origin and heavenly in its character.

And have we not now reached the Millennium? That golden age to which the Church has always looked forward, in which its brightest hopes for the children of men are to be realized? Is this not it? What less can it be? The Church honored as the Lamb's wife, beautiful in the white linen of her righteousness, ruling over a world in which there is no longer ignorance of the Bible, spurious religion, beastly misgovernment, misrepresentation of the truth, human opposer, or Satan walking about as a roaring lion, seeking whom he may devour! Surely it would be hard to imagine any conditions very much superior to these for Christian usefulness, and Christian happiness, and for universal well-being.

There are those, of course, who would add to this picture the personal presence of the Saviour in the world as a visible king over His people. But the difficulties of such a view are insuperable. Such a feature would certainly be introduced with more emphasis into the description than in the quite indirect manner in which it must, if at all, be detected. The second coming of our Lord is too great an occurrence, and is constantly represented in the New Testament as too majestic a demonstration, to be supposed to have taken place at this point with so little to indicate it. If the binding of Satan was worthy to be described so dramatically, why not the far greater event of the reappearance of Jesus upon the earth?

The second coming of our Lord is, indeed, to be found in this chapter, but it is after the Millennium instead of before it. The occupant of the great white throne which is set for judgment must be He, for He told His disciples that the Father had committed all judgment unto the Son. But the throne is not set and the books are not opened until the thousand years have passed, and Satan has escaped out of his prison, and Gog and Magog have fought and been vanquished. It is out of the question to find any premillennial advent of Jesus here.

He reigns, indeed, during the Millennium most truly and grandly over the earth, but it is in and through His people. The emphasis is all upon the human representatives of His sovereignty. "I saw thrones, and *they* sat upon them, and judgment was given unto *them*." Surely the authority of King Jesus will be none the less impressive and wonderful that He exercises it through His redeemed people instead of by reappearing bodily upon earth. The master who in his absence is none the less master than in his presence with his servants is a master indeed. The Christians of the Millennium will not need watching. They will be like " that faithful and wise servant" whom his lord can "find so doing," though he come at any time he pleases. The grandeur of this period is enhanced by the very fact that the people of God will still "walk by faith and not by sight," and yet "reign with Christ" as really as if He were visibly present with them. The necessity of His visible presence would be a sensible detraction from the spiritual glory of the millennial age.

Another great misconception of this period which would vastly diminish its spiritual splendor is that the sovereigns represented as enthroned are the *martyrs* of the Church only. When the martyrs enjoy peculiar honor and influence, will not the whole Church share that honor and influence? It is impossible to imagine a situation which would be pre-eminently advantageous to those who have been "beheaded for the testimony of Jesus and for the Word of God," which would not be also very advantageous for every true disciple. But the prophecy does not limit the good here described to the martyrs only. It is for all "such as worshipped not the beast, neither his image, and received not the mark upon their forehead and upon their hand." This includes all real Christians. Of the faithful of all ages it must in some way be true that "they lived and reigned with Christ a thousand years."

This being settled, it is obvious that we cannot interpret the language "the first resurrection" literally. The general resurrection of the just we are elsewhere taught to expect at the same time as that of the unjust. We have not yet reached the point where death is to be literally abolished for Christ's people by being cast into the lake of fire. During the thousand years of this period Christians must be supposed to grow old and die as before. Would their death be consistent with a state of things in which the sainted dead of former generations were living upon the earth in resurrection bodies? The supposition is too incongruous to be seriously entertained. Nor is it necessary to entertain it. We escape instantly from any apparent necessity of entertaining it by remembering that here, as elsewhere in this book, we are dealing with symbolism which, taken literally, hides the very truths which it is intended to disclose.

"The first resurrection," then, must be a figure by which the superior glory of the millennial state is suggested. It will be *as if* the martyrs had risen from their graves and seated themselves in the places of earthly power and dignity. So great will be the contrast between the millennial age and former ages, that the kind of persons formerly most hated and abused will be the very class most loved and obeyed. It is impossible to imagine a greater revolution. The martyrs lost their lives because the world did not understand them, and "was not worthy of them." They were victims of the deceit, ignorance, vice, superstition, and tyranny which made their times so dark. But the time which we are contemplating is to be the exact opposite of all this. The martyr character will then be so thoroughly understood, so highly appreciated, so warmly loved, so faithfully reproduced, that it will live, and flourish, and reign all over the earth. Will not that be the best possible millennium, and will not the situation of the Church be worthy to be described as "the first resurrection"?

Alford vehemently protests against such an interpretation on the ground that "the first resurrection" is so called in contrast with that of the "rest of the dead," who "lived not until the thousand years should be finished." He says that if "the first resurrection may be understood to mean spiritual rising with Christ, while the second means literal rising from the grave, then there is an end to all significance in language, and Scripture is wiped out as a definite testimony to anything. If the first resurrection is spiritual, then so is the second, which I suppose *none will be hardy enough to maintain.*" Alford is very warm, but the conception which he scouts as too preposterous to be considered appears to me the only proper interpretation. So thinks Dr. Justin A. Smith and so thinks Dr. Alvah Hovey. There is really no difficulty about making both resurrections spiritual. The spiritual resurrection of the martyrs is the period during which they will be honored and imitated. The spiritual resurrection of the "rest of the dead"—that is, of the wicked dead, will be that strange outbreak of sin and violence which is announced as to take place at the close of the millennium. When Gog and Magog come forth from the four corners of the earth, as the sand of the sea in multitude, to compass the camp of the saints and the beloved city, it will be *as if* all the bad emperors, and all the wicked popes, and all the bloodthirsty inquisitors had risen from their graves and covered the "breadth of the earth" with their polluting, destroying legions. With such a conception before the inspiring Mind, no wonder it exclaimed, "Blessed and holy is he that hath part in the *first* resurrection; over these the second death hath no power; but they shall be priests of God and of Christ, and shall reign with Him a thousand years."

That any one should take the "thousand years" literally seems very strange to one who has recognized the thoroughly symbolical character of the whole book. It is no less symbolic in its use of numbers than it is in other respects. In fact, it is the *numbers* of the Apocalypse which all would most easily perceive to be symbolic. Nobody, perhaps, would take the "sevens" of this book literally, and few would imagine the days, hours, and months literal periods. Why should this thousand years be an exception to the general rule? There is no good reason for so regarding it. The attempt to compute the age of the world by an estimate, into which the millennial period enters as a literal thousand years, is a mathematical conjecture from which nothing can be expected, because one of the chief quantities of the problem is utterly indefinite.

This, however, may be said, that the evident intention of inspiration is to assure us that the era of righteousness will be exceedingly protracted, of a duration whose length in terms of earthly years seems bewilderingly extended. For if the period of evil, during which the enemies of God have the upper hand in the world, is represented by the short time of forty-and-two months, or twelve hundred and sixty days, or three and one-half years, then how long will the period of good last, which is represented by a thousand years, to carry out the proportion between the numbers? The period of evil is not yet over, and will not be until the papacy, worldly powers, and false teachers are all out of the way. If our two thousand years of struggle with adverse influences be called three and one-half years in the prophecy, how long will be the reign of the saints represented by one thousand years? It is indisputable that this number stands for a duration of the kingdom of light immensely great, so great as almost to take one's breath away in its contemplation. Those who are ciphering out the speedy end of the world can find no aid or comfort here. It will be as it ought to be; the time of the wicked will be comparatively short upon the earth, and the time of the good will be inconceivably extended. God will not build up His earthly empire and then immediately destroy it. It will last as good things can last and ought to last; last long enough to show that, in spite of all the cunning of the wicked, it is the meek who "inherit the earth."

That such a protracted period of righteousness would be followed by even a temporary reaction we should not suppose had we not an explicit prediction of the event. That Satan should ever get loose again, and, being loose, should find anywhere in the millennial world anybody to deceive and use for his base purposes, is not certainly a fact which we should anticipate. But thus, we are informed, it is to be. The fair earth, bright with the light of Christian knowledge, is to be darkened by one more spiritual eclipse; the broad empire of Jesus is to produce one more insurrection. The myrmidons of the devil are to muster from every corner of the earth, and be arrayed in countless numbers against the righteous government of the Church and against all her holy institutions. Where such hordes can come from we could not imagine did we not remember that human nature must always remain the same, and that every oncoming generation would sweep Christianity from the globe were it not met and transformed by the converting power of the Holy Spirit. Any remissness on the part of Christian people, any over-confidence produced by a long period of security, would permit a generation of unconverted children to grow up, who would soon reverse the whole situation. A possibility like this is sufficient to remove the incredulity which we naturally feel at the prediction of that unholy war which the world is to see even after it has enjoyed its symbolic thousand years of " righteousness, and peace, and joy in the Holy Ghost."

How long this era of misrule is to last we have no hint, but the natural impression of the story is that the triumph of the wicked will be short. It needed but this one more struggle with evil to complete the education of the Church in this direction and finish its probation. It needed but this one more opportunity for the Devil and his servants to fill up the cup of their iniquity, and to reach the doom prepared for them. The frenzy of a rebellion against the peace and order of the millennial state. is not only the last, but the worst exhibition of what sin and sinners are capable of doing. In proportion to the moral grandeur of that Christian civilization whose beauty and blessedness will have perpetuated themselves by their very excellence for a period almost unlimited will appear the depravity of that causeless and inexcusable insurrection which could be willing to swallow up so much happiness. Such gigantic criminality will loudly call for divine judgments, and will receive them. The wrath of God will smite the offenders with His heaviest thunderbolts, and, as of old, the righteous will have only to stand still and see the salvation of God. The Arch-adversary will be put where he can do no more mischief, and can forever only writhe in the torment of his impotent malice.

We have now reached the last scene in the history of our present dispensation. It winds up with the coming of Christ in His glory, the general resurrection, and the Judgment Day. What events are these to complete the education of the Church, and to fit God's people for everlasting blessedness! If anything were lacking in our human outfit for a happy eternity, surely it would be supplied on this last great day. What shall we not *know* which we need to know when the *books* are opened which contain those final disclosures? There will not then remain any ignorance in any sanctified mind that will lessen its usefulness or endanger its happiness. At the time that the sea and Hades give up their dead, and they that are alive are caught up to meet the Lord in the air, we may say that the world is now perfectly illuminated, and all that was promised in the first chapter of Revelation is now fully accomplished.

XX.

THE NEW JERUSALEM.

The process of the illumination of our race having been completed by the disclosures of the Judgment Day, the proper termination of the Apocalypse would seem to be a symbolic representation of the grand result accomplished. That is precisely what we have in the twenty-first and twenty-second chapters of the book. Its end seems just what our theory of its interpretation requires. These last chapters show the *world lighted;* the glorious education of the saved race of man in its magnificent completeness.

Even those who have the least notion of the general tenor of the prophecy cannot help seeing the blaze of splendor which bursts forth from the final chapters. Whether it be the splendor of the Church on earth or of the glorified in heaven a casual reader might be uncertain, but of one thing he might be sure, that everything on earth that is brightest is used to heighten the description. Its principal characteristic is *light.* The holy Jerusalem is seen "descending out of heaven, having the *glory of God,* and *her light* is like unto a stone most precious, even like a *jasper* stone, *clear as crystal.*" "And the building of the wall of it was *jasper;* and the city was pure gold, like unto *clear glass.*" "And the city had no need of the sun, neither of the moon to shine in it, for the glory of

God did *lighten* it, and the Lamb is the *light* thereof." "And the nations of them that are saved shall walk in the *light* of it." "There shall be *no night* there." "And there shall be *no night* there; and they need no candle, neither light of the sun; for the Lord God giveth them *light*."

One has only to read these words and to remember that the first chapter of the book was a display of the luminaries by means of which it was proposed to light up the world, to feel that the fulfilment of their promise is now exhibited. The world is seen actually lighted. Night has given place to everlasting day. The new earth needs neither sun, nor moon, nor artificial lamp, because it has become self-luminous, being interpenetrated everywhere by the glory of God.

The more we dwell upon the terms used to describe the New Jerusalem, the more we shall perceive this wonderful transformation. The glory of God which blazes forth from the city is that supernal splendor which Moses saw in the burning bush and Solomon in the temple; which shone around the shepherds at the birth of Christ, and caused the noonday of Damascus to pale before it. The jasper stone, clear as crystal, is the very jewel chosen to represent the softened radiance of the divine Sun early in this same book. The very walls of this city are jasper, and its foundations precious stones in all the colors of the rainbow, these symbols of God having now become the symbols of the Church. Even the golden streets are clear as glass, by which is evidently meant that there is no part of the glorified Church which is not purified from all taint of darkness and permeated by the light of God. The once opaque earth, hiding in its bosom the darkness of midnight and having no light except as it received it from some foreign source, is now become itself a luminary, able to shed light on other orbs. Among all the stars and suns which glitter in the concave above us, none can seem so magnificent a light-bearer as this holy city which John saw descending from heaven.

The question arises, Is this the description of saved humanity in heaven, or are we to understand by it the future of our own planet after it has been purified by fire and so reconstructed that it is fit to be the dwelling-place of a perfected race? Most commentators seem to cling to the latter idea. So careful and spiritual an interpreter as Dr. Justin A. Smith quite endorses the notion that these last chapters of the Apocalypse not only picture to us a spiritual state, but contain hints of the later geography of the globe. He is willing to take literally the statement that there is to be "no more sea." Alford struggles with the statement that the height of the city was equal to its enormous length and breadth, and after calling Düsterdieck's view that the houses were three hundred and seventy-five miles high "too absurd" to be considered, gives his own, that together with the mountain on which the city stood it was three hundred and seventy-five miles high, which he evidently regards as a reasonable estimate. It seems to me that such interpretations furnish the *reductio ad absurdum* of the attempt to find in this description the geography of the earth after the Judgment Day.

An earth with no sea, and therefore with no rivers, rivulets, lakes, fountains, wells, clouds, or water; an earth with mountains three hundred and seventy-five miles high would be an earth so different from the present one as to be practically a different place altogether. I cannot imagine any object for which the glorified saints would desire to return to such a place. Certainly there would be nothing familiar about it, nor does it seem to our minds nearly so beautiful and attractive as our present earth. The suggested changes are such as to remind us of what astronomers say to be the present condition of the moon, a huge excoriated cinder, with nothing left but its ugly burned bones. To imagine the sanctified children of earth, who have dwelt for a while in the heavenly mansions, to have to come back to such an earth, which their recollections of its former fairness would make seem all the more dreary, is anything but a conception of heightened happiness. The naturalized inhabitants of heaven would not be likely to relish an invitation to return to any earth any more than a well-to-do Irishman in America would relish an invitation to return to the peat-bogs and mud cabins of the Emerald Isle.

No; it is impossible to take the symbolism of these last chapters of the Revelation with any degree of literalness. Dr. Smith quotes Stuart approvingly where he says, regarding the loftiness of the New Jerusalem, "We are relieved by calling to mind that all is symbol." Precisely. But it is as difficult to find anything but symbol in one place as in another. It is as dangerous to look for topography in the first item as in the last.

What is it that is symbolized? The final, glorified state of the Church. Where in the universe that Church is to be this vision gives us not the slightest hint, except that it will be in heaven. The earth which is described is not the material earth, but the spiritual one. Wherever the saved inhabitants of this planet finally dwell, there will be a new earth, as the residence of the Pilgrim Fathers on this continent made here a *New* England. The people of this globe are the most important part of it, and when it has been so desiccated by fire as to have no more sea in it, the real earth will be where *they* are and not where it is.

" *A new heaven* and a new earth." Let us not forget that the heaven is to be a new one as well as the earth. Will not heaven be a new place when earth, the people of earth, are brought into it? The heaven where the four-and-twenty elders sit upon their four-and-twenty thrones, and the blood-washed multitude sing the new song, is essentially a different place from what it was before their admission. The great change in the new heaven and the new earth from the old heaven and the old earth is that they are brought into such close relation. "There is no more *sea*." The sea is the symbol of separation. I think not of the ocean of water which divides Europe from America, but of that ocean of space which divides planet from planet, and star from star, and earth from heaven. That sea will be no more when earth and heaven are brought into actual juxtaposition. The earth will be in heaven. The same blessed truth is suggested by the towering up of the New Jerusalem three hundred and seventy-five miles into the sky. When we can get up as far as that we can get clear up. Heaven and earth will have met at the top of that mountain.

The same thing is hinted in the statement that the New Jerusalem is "made ready as a *bride* adorned for her *husband*." Husbands and wives generally live together, and when the great King marries His earthly bride He will probably take her to His palace and His capital. He will not go to the humbler abode.

Removal of all *separation!* This is the thought which is repeated again and again. "And I heard a great voice of the throne saying, Behold, the tabernacle of God is *with men*, and He shall *dwell* with them, and they shall be His people, and God Himself shall be *with them*, their God; and He shall wipe away every tear from their eyes; and *death* shall be no more, neither shall there be mourning, nor crying, nor pain any more; the first things are passed away." It is impossible to conceive of this total revolution in an earthly situation. Even through the millennial ages death is represented as continuing on the globe. It is not finally cast into the lake of fire until the resurrection morning. But when the saints are "caught up to meet the Lord in the air, to be forever with the Lord," all death and all sorrow seem forever precluded.

The character of the people who are to constitute this new earth is stated in such terms as to harmonize with the symbolism. The symbol is a city transparent in every part and radiant with the light of God. This means, of course, perfect knowledge, perfect sincerity, and perfect purity. Twice the character of the inhabitants of the city is indicated by a contrast, the climax of which is that they *are not liars*, they do not make a *lie*. They are such that the nations can walk in the light of their teaching and example. The kings of the earth bring their glory and honor into this city, and the glory and honor of the nations are brought into it. This, I suppose, means the real kings, not the titular kings, and the real glory and honor, not the sham and shabby glory. The real kings of the earth are its teachers, the rulers of its best thought, and the greatest glory of man, the Bible tells us, is to know God. All the items of this description harmonize with the symbols, and set before our minds a human society no longer stumbling in the darkness of ignorance and sin, but walking in the light of life and of heaven.

The last picture of the book is the description of a spiritual paradise. Through the midst of the city flows " a river of water of life, bright as crystal, proceeding out of the throne of God and of the Lamb." This river washes the roots of the trees of life upon its banks, and keeps them perennially green and fruitful. Nothing seems to me stranger than the fact that no commentator whom I have read, not even the most spiritual, has here thought of the Holy Spirit as the reality symbolized by this crystal stream. Yet nothing could be more natural than such a thought. Water is widely employed in the Scriptures as a symbol of the Holy Spirit. The Gospel of John explains the living water to be the Holy Spirit. The good man of the first psalm, who meditates in the inspired law, is like a tree planted by a river of water. The stream which Ezekiel saw coming forth from the threshold of the temple and deepening as it ran until it gave life to the Dead Sea is undoubtedly the Holy Spirit. Here the water proceeds from the throne of God and of the Lamb, which represents the procession of the Holy Spirit from the Father and the Son.

And if we ask what is to maintain the sanctified Church in the enjoyment of its exalted privileges, what is the answer but the Holy Spirit? "He shall teach you all things" is to be as true of heaven as of earth. "They shall be all taught of God" as well there as here. There, as here, He will lead the saints of God "into all truth," and because they have Him for their constant guide and instructor, they will constantly advance and never retrograde.

Have we not reached the last possible suggestion of the final goodness and glory of the redeemed? If they have the holy Spirit in perpetual enjoyment, they will bear the "fruit of the Spirit." They will bear "twelve manner of fruits," which must mean all kinds of fruits which are possible to that combination of the divine and human natures which is represented by twelve, the product of the divine number, three, by the human number, four. That the leaves of these trees of life are to be for "the healing of the nations" may serve dimly to suggest to us the influence for good in this universe of the people whom God will have saved from the evil of earth and associated with Himself in the most intimate and blessed partnership which can exist between the Creator and any of His creatures. "They shall see His face; His name shall be in their foreheads; . . . they shall reign forever and ever."

As I close these studies in the Apocalypse I am impelled to bear my testimony to the fulness of its inspiration. It seems to me the most wonderful prophecy of the Bible. Both the themes which it treats and the manner in which it treats them are far beyond mere human art. Renan's pitiful slur that this book is the product of petty malignity among the apostles could never be uttered by any one who had any worthy conception of the contents of the book. It is like a spiritual telescope put to the eye of the reader, enabling him to behold the most distant scenes in time and in space. How wide its scope! How far its outlook! How grand its theme! How inspiring its revelations! It is exactly what it needs to be to occupy its place in the canon, to be the final word of the revealing Mind, and, in some respects, its grandest.

One who attempts to comment upon this book cannot fail to feel its warning against any addition to the prophecy or subtraction from it. I ask myself if I have thus drawn upon myself "the plagues that are written in this book." My thought has been neither to add to nor to take from; I have studied and written with the profoundest reverence in my heart, and the desire to let the words of God produce their own impression upon my mind. It is with the hope that I have contributed to the knowledge of my readers that which will make the Apocalypse to them the same treasury of blessed information that it has become to me, that I have written these pages. If those who read them feel as I feel, I am sure I shall have done them or the book no harm. My heart glows with a brighter hope, and is nerved with a more cheerful courage and a stronger determination, as I think of those bright and happy views of the world's future which I have gained from the Apocalypse.

The "coming" of which it discourses is, first and chiefly, the coming of Christ as *the Truth*. As we see how much that means, what consequences it involves, we are impelled to join in the prayer of the book, "Lord Jesus, come quickly!" So He promises to come; and considered with reference to the work to be done and the tremendous difficulties to be encountered, the coming is quick, though it seems to us to be so slow. Doubtless the latter stages of its progress will be far more rapid. When broad foundations have been laid and the way thoroughly prepared the Lord will hasten His coming.

Thank God, we may all share in the vast benefits which this book pictures. As we see their greatness and grandeur, they seem too much for such creatures as we are to obtain. But they are freely offered to us all. "*Whosoever will*, let him take the water of life freely!" Oh, that an intelligent view of the blessedness disclosed in the Apocalypse, as the possible portion of every child of man, may move every soul to an immediate and grateful acceptance of the gift!

www.ingramcontent.com/pod-product-compliance
Lightning Source LLC
Chambersburg PA
CBHW031831230426
43669CB00009B/1308